T0356163

Marci Baker

The Quilt Binding
BIBLE

25 Flawless Finishes
Techniques &
Troubleshooting

C&T PUBLISHING
Another Maker Inspired!

Text copyright © 2025 by Marci Baker

Photography and artwork copyright © 2025 by C&T Publishing, Inc.

PUBLISHER: Amy Barrett-Daffin
CREATIVE DIRECTOR: Gailen Runge
SENIOR EDITOR: Roxane Cerda
TECHNICAL EDITOR: Kathryn Patterson
COVER/BOOK DESIGNER: April Mostek
PRODUCTION COORDINATOR: Tim Manibusan
ILLUSTRATORS: Marci Baker, Mary Flynn, Zinnia Heinzmann, Tim Manibusan
PHOTOGRAPHY COORDINATOR: Rachel Ackley
FRONT COVER PHOTOGRAPHY by C&T Publishing
PHOTOGRAPHY by C&T Publishing, unless otherwise noted
Published by C&T Publishing, Inc., P.O. Box 1456, Lafayette, CA 94549

All rights reserved. No part of this work covered by the copyright hereon may be used in any form or reproduced by any means—graphic, electronic, or mechanical, including photocopying, recording, taping, or information storage and retrieval systems—without written permission from the publisher. The copyrights on individual artworks are retained by the artists as noted in *The Quilt Binding Bible*. These designs may be used to make items for personal use only and may not be used for the purpose of personal profit. Items created to benefit nonprofit groups, or that will be publicly displayed, must be conspicuously labeled with the following credit: "Designs copyright © 2025 by Marci Baker from the book *The Quilt Binding Bible* from C&T Publishing, Inc." Permission for all other purposes must be requested in writing from C&T Publishing, Inc.

Attention Teachers: C&T Publishing, Inc., encourages the use of our books as texts for teaching. You can find lesson plans for many of our titles at ctpub.com or contact us at ctinfo@ctpub.com.

We take great care to ensure that the information included in our products is accurate and presented in good faith, but no warranty is provided, nor are results guaranteed. Having no control over the choices of materials or procedures used, neither the author nor C&T Publishing, Inc., shall have any liability to any person or entity with respect to any loss or damage caused directly or indirectly by the information contained in this book. For your convenience, we post an up-to-date listing of corrections on our website (ctpub.com). If a correction is not already noted, please contact our customer service department at ctinfo@ctpub.com or P.O. Box 1456, Lafayette, CA 94549.

Trademark (™) and registered trademark (®) names are used throughout this book. Rather than use the symbols with every occurrence of a trademark or registered trademark name, we are using the names only in the editorial fashion and to the benefit of the owner, with no intention of infringement.

Library of Congress Cataloging-in-Publication Data

Names: Baker, Marcia L., author.

Title: The quilt binding bible : 25 flawless finishes; techniques &

troubleshooting / by Marci Baker.

Description: Lafayette, CA : C&T Publishing Inc., [2025] | Summary: "Need to bind a quilt and don't recall the steps? Looking for a unique binding to set your quilt apart? Included inside are 25 binding techniques with step-by-step instructions, tips, and troubleshooting hacks for any quilt binding need"-- Provided by publisher.

Identifiers: LCCN 2024030836 | ISBN 9781644035214 (trade paperback) | ISBN 9781644035221 (ebook)

Subjects: LCSH: Quilting--Patterns. | BISAC: CRAFTS & HOBBIES / Patchwork |

CRAFTS & HOBBIES / Sewing

Classification: LCC TT835 .B2586 2025 | DDC 746.46/041--dc23/eng/20240806

LC record available at https://lccn.loc.gov/2024030836

Printed in China

10 9 8 7 6 5 4 3 2 1

Dedication

To Sara Nephew: You are an inspirational role model, a patient mentor, and a true friend. You have blessed me in so many ways—thank you!

Acknowledgments

Thank you to Joen Wolfrom who inspired my joining strips instructions with her design technique in *Landscapes & Illusions*.

Thank you to Sandee Heldt of Quiltn' at the General Store in Kentucky, who is an outstanding teacher, quilter, and seamstress, for the tailoring tips and tricks.

I would like to thank the following manufacturers who provided top-notch supplies for the samples and videos associated with this book:

Moda Fabrics: Bella Solids used for most samples

In the Beginning: A Year of Art, inspiration for samples

Quilter's Dream Batting

Presencia: threads including 60 wt and 50 wt cotton, Finca Mouline embroidery thread, and perle cotton

Taylor Seville Originals: notions

Wonderfil: Invisafil 100.wt polyester thread, IF718, used for quilting most samples

CONTENTS

INTRO DUCTION

"Binding, YES, finally!" or "Oh no!" Which is your reaction?
Some quilters love it, but I would venture to say that a majority of us have
seen it as a hurdle to jump. Whenever it is time to bind a quilt, I am usually
in a hurry. Early on in my quilting life, I would hunt for a book that had
some instructions, muddle through it, and be glad to have it done even
though it wasn't necessarily the neatest. A few months later I would be
back in the same situation, wondering when I would ever learn binding,
really learn it.

By chance I had the opportunity to study the process. One of the projects
in this book is The Quilter's Pocketbook (page 130). In one year, I made
more than 100 of them! My brain was analyzing: "This one doesn't look
good, what went wrong?" or "This one looks great, why?" From this
experience, I mastered and truly learned how to easily apply binding,
miter corners, and join the ends, successfully. And I know what causes the
problems. Now I can share all those tips with you!

Video Tutorials The process for finishing the edge of the
quilt is three-dimensional. Communicating and understanding
the concept with only a two-dimensional drawing, with no
action, can be challenging. I've created videos where you can
view and understand many processes in more detail. Visit C&T
Publishing's YouTube Channel and search for "binding" to see
my growing library of videos. youtube.com/@CandTPublishing

I have used this basic process as a springboard to try variations in width of strips, adding in piping, developing facing techniques, and imagining and trying many possibilities. There's always more than one way to bind a quilt, and with so many to choose from, how do we decide? If you are in a hurry-got-to-get-it-done mode, turn to Go-To Basic Double Fold Binding (page 50) where I have the step-by-step reference for basic binding, finished by hand or by machine. If you are looking to try something new, I have put together a Pros and Cons table (page 12). The table includes photos of the finishes, a level of challenge, a list of niceties, a list of the drawbacks, and the page number for the binding so you can get more detail. From the information in the Pros and Cons table, you can choose a method that will be the perfect finish for your current creation.

All of these require some basic knowledge for selecting the grain, figuring yardage, cutting strips, joining the strips, and more, to set the stage for success. If you have varied results with these steps, read through and find those elusive details that can now make the process easier and the results more satisfying. If you are confident with this part of the process, feel free to jump right into selecting the binding.

As you flip through the pages, it's apparent that there are some mathematical equations. For those who are faint of heart when it comes to math, know that it is simple math with well-defined terms. Take a deep breath, take it step by step, and all will be fine. To double check the math, ask yourself if the yardage amount makes sense for the project; make a binding sample to see if you're getting the look you want. You will have confidence in your efforts.

Perfection or Finished? Personally, I like a nice finish. That is why I figured out what matters on so many quilting processes. However, sometimes my binding may not be perfect, depending on the machine, the fabrics, my mood, etc. If the binding finishes the edge in a neat way, I am satisfied. Knowing this, you can imagine that I am not one to spend hours for a perfect project. And so it is with the samples in this book. In general, on my projects I use thread that matches the fabric so it doesn't show. However, on these samples, I have used contrasting thread so that you can see the stitches and better understand how they are made. You may notice stitches that aren't the straightest, or the most even. Different machines provide different results. I used three different machines while working on this book!

Why am I bothering to tell you this? Not to point out where I didn't get the best result, but to give you permission to not stress over your own possible imperfections. With practice the process gets easier and the results get better.

The first methods given use the quilt top and backing for the finishing. No extra fabric is required. These are often used as beginner techniques. However, they have the drawback of a less than desirable wearability and can be challenging to make look nice, especially for the less experienced quilter.

Then we move to traditional bindings and variations on the theme. These styles include double fold, single fold, striped, pieced, wide, miniature, curved, matched, scallops, and facing, each with step-by-step illustrated instructions. After this, you'll find special instances like mitered corners for different angles.

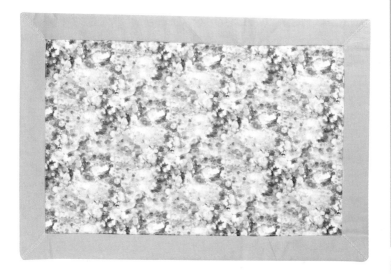

The third and fourth sections cover methods for adding an extra special touch. A flourish to the finish could include piping, a flange of color, or decorative items like lace being inserted between the quilt and the binding. Design elements such as prairie points, ruffles, or petals can be extensions of the quilt.

For the opportunity to try some of the different options, I have included some quick projects (beginning on page 130).

In this compendium of binding techniques, I describe in detail the steps for each. This is just the beginning though. Once you have the knowledge of these methods, you can make them your own and create that perfect finish for your own personal style—a true signature for your works of art and heart.

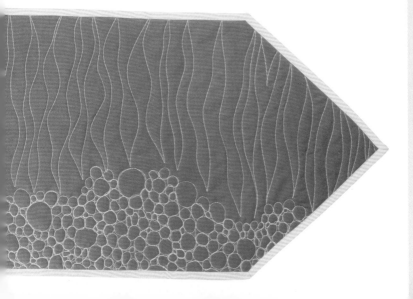

PROS AND CONS LISTING

BINDING TYPE (PAGE NUMBER)	EXPERIENCE LEVEL	GRAIN: STRAIGHT OR BIAS	LONG WEARING?
SELF BINDING (31)	Beginner	Straight	No
TURNED (PILLOWCASE, ENVELOPE) (38)	Beginner	N/A	No
KNIFE EDGE (46)	Beginner	Straight	No
DOUBLE FOLD OR FRENCH (50)	Beginner	Either	Yes
SINGLE FOLD (64)	Intermediate	Either	No
STRIPED (66)	Intermediate	Both	N/A
PIECED (69)	Advanced	Either	No
WIDE (70)	Intermediate	Either	Yes, if double fold. No, if single fold
MINIATURE—⅛″ (72)	Advanced	Bias	Yes
MINIATURE—¹⁄₁₆″ (74)	Advanced	Bias	No
ARTIST'S (76)	Intermediate	Bias	No

Here you will find information on each type of finish.
The name, a close-up, best uses, limitations, wearability, and other considerations. Hopefully your decision-making process will be easier. No matter which one you choose, before cutting all the binding or trimming the quilt edges, I recommend making a sample piece using the fabrics and batting of the project to be sure the results will be as expected.

PROS	CONS
Simple, easy finish that requires no extra fabric, just enough backing to do the trick.	Only one layer of fabric, it may wear out quickly, If worn, requires binding.
Easy to do on small pieces. Edge is finished before quilting. Also good for tied quilts, medium size.	Edge of front and back fabric will wear. If worn, no seam allowance to apply binding, quilt border or design will be covered by binding.
Gives the edge a clean look with no binding applied. Can be finished by hand or machine.	Edge of front and back fabric will wear. If worn, no seam allowance to apply binding, quilt border or design will be covered by binding. Extra time needed for edges to align and look neat.
Sturdiest and easier to apply than most other methods.	Compared to single fold, uses more fabric.
Less fabric required than double fold.	Pressing requires some time. Only one layer of fabric, it may wear out quickly, requiring rebinding. The last fold can be challenging to keep straight unless it is pressed well.
Adds extra flair to the finished quilt. Is paired with single fold or double fold binding, see related pros.	Is paired with single fold or double fold binding, see related cons.
Scrappy, fun finish can use fabrics from quilt top.	Extra effort required to create the binding. More difficult because seams might pull apart when applying. When paired with double fold, method creates bulk at each seam.
Good for large quilts, placemats, or adding a strong design on smaller pieces. The width of the binding can finish the project nicely.	Takes more fabric. Needs additional planning to plot widths on front and back and get correct alignment.
A sturdy finish for garments and quilts. Perfect scale for wallhangings, too.	Needs care at mitered corners and trimmed seam allowances.
Excellent finish for miniature quilts, scaled-down design, detailed work.	Requires attention to every detail as it is fine work. Not a sturdy finish. Use only on pieces that will not be handled significantly.
Results in a clean edge with no visible binding. Uses less fabric than double fold.	Adds bulk to the edges unless seam allowances are graded. Quilt edges can wear requiring binding which cuts into the design.

BINDING TYPE (PAGE NUMBER)	EXPERIENCE LEVEL	GRAIN: STRAIGHT OR BIAS	LONG WEARING?
CURVED (80)	Intermediate	Bias	Yes, if double fold. No, if single fold
MATCHED (82)	Intermediate/ Advanced	Either	Yes, if double fold. No, if single fold
PIECED AT CORNER (84)	Intermediate/ Advanced	Either	No
FACING (86)	Intermediate	Straight	No
SCALLOPS (97)	Intermediate/ Advanced	Bias	Yes, if double fold. No, if single fold
FLANGE (100)	Intermediate	Either	Yes
FAUX FLANGE (102)	Intermediate	Straight	Yes
BINDING WITH PIPING (104)	Intermediate	Either, bias for piping	Yes
LACE / TATTING (107)	Intermediate	Either	No
PIPING ON THE EDGE (114)	Intermediate	Bias	No
PRAIRIE POINTS (116)	Intermediate/ Advanced	Either	No
RUFFLES (123)	Advanced	Straight	No
PETALS (126)	Intermediate/ Advanced	N/A	No

PROS	CONS
Expands design options to include curved edges.	Must use bias strips. Width is limited based on amount of curve. Easing and stretching required to get flat results.
Creates a seamless finish while allowing for the durability of an applied binding.	Time and planning must be spent to create seamless transitions with the design.
Cool look.	A lot of seams in one place, so it can be bulky. Requres some practice to get the desired result.
Good way to finish irregular edges like hexagons, double wedding ring, curves, art designs, etc.	Can use large amounts of fabric depending on the design. Requires clipping and careful turning. Adds bulk to edges unless seam allowances are graded. Quilt edges can wear requiring binding which cuts into the design.
On the right quilt, creates an elegant finish. Since it is bound, it is a durable edge.	Need to plan for desired shape and even spacing. Inside corners are mitered.
Wonderful way to add color at the edge of the quilt. Fairly easy and worth the effort for special effect.	Applied in two steps.
Easy to accomplish this look with two strips sewn together lengthwise.	Cutting two fabrics for the binding. Try different combinations to get desired result.
Wonderful way to add color and dimension at the edge of the quilt.	Requires zipper foot.
The perfect finish for the right quilt.	Want to be sure it accents the quilt rather than detracts. Two step process.
Just a touch of color at the very edge of the quilt.	Requires zipper foot. Easing around curved corners to get flat finish. When worn, replacement will cut into the quilt design.
Just the right touch on some quilts. Worth the effort for the right quilt. Good for quilts that are meant to be decorative.	Takes time to plan, cut, fold, and press points. When worn, replacement will cut into the quilt design.
Perfect for a little girl's quilt or other special quilt.	The extra weight will cause wear. Uses significant amount of fabric for the ruffle.
A unique finish that can add just the right touch. A way to have curved edges without binding or facing curves.	Extra time needed to make the petals. When worn, replacement will cut into the quilt design.

A FEW
BASICS

There are some general principles that apply to all these binding techniques. Most important is to try the concept by making a small sample so any fine tuning can be done for guaranteed success. This chapter discusses information about setting up the sewing machine, figuring yardage, cutting different grains of fabric, joining strips together, pressing, and more. You may be familiar with these concepts. Or you may find a solution to common mysteries, like what causes that "elbow" in a strip, or why the strips are staggered when they are joined together. Read through and find the details you need to achieve your best finish.

Make a Sample Binding

Each of these finishes is affected by the fabrics, batting, machine setup, and operator's technique. The directions work as written. However, with all these variables, adjustments may be needed to get the desired result. The most important advice that I have for your success is to make a small sample, 5˝ long, plus a corner if needed, to test the process. Use the same materials as the project. Change the strip width, the amount of batting trimmed, or the alignment of the quilt with the sewing machine, i.e. the seam allowance, to get the results that you want. This sample will be worth the effort!

Set Up Your Sewing Machine

- Set up your machine with a walking foot, even-feed foot, or the configuration recommended by the manufacturer.

- For some machines, you can lessen the pressure on the presser foot, allowing the top to move with the batting and backing.

- If possible, move the needle over so the edge of the quilt is aligned with the edge of the foot. This way, all the feed dogs are pulling the fabric through.

- Support the quilt around the machine so it does not drag. Make sure the next 8˝–12˝ of the quilt are loose to keep the quilt from shifting when the needle is raised.

- When applying the binding, stop with the needle down before adjusting the quilt.

- If the quilting is not to the edge of the quilt, before trimming, machine baste the layers together with a setting of 3.0mm or 8 spi (stitches per inch), in the seam allowance.

- Use an edge to help guide the quilt for a consistent seam allowance and a straight binding. I recommend *Sewing Edge*, a thick vinyl strip that can be positioned where needed for any size seam allowance.

TAKE CONTROL When working with a project of any size, it can be challenging to move the bulk of the quilt hanging off the side of the machine bed. One tool that I have found indispensable is a pair of quilting gloves that are made for moving the quilt around when machine quilting. This allows me to have control and to guide the quilt during the binding process rather than trying to grab the quilt and push or pull it through the machine. I prefer gloves with the thumb and forefinger missing so that I can work with scissors and thread easily.

Grain: Bias vs. Straight

Grain is the direction of the weave of the fabric. The amount of stretch can make binding easier. Lengthwise grain (unwrapping from the bolt) has very little stretch. Crosswise grain (the width of the fabric) has some stretch. Bias is any direction that is not on the two grains. This has significant stretch with the most being the true bias, at a 45-degree diagonal.

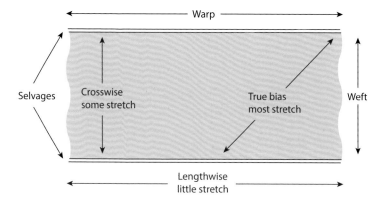

Bias has more wearability than lengthwise or crosswise grain. Here's why: Consider fabric folded in half on lengthwise or crosswise grain. Imagine there are 100 threads per inch on that fold. As the fabric wears, the threads break down. In that inch, 100 threads will need to break before a significant hole appears. And if something catches in that hole, the fabric could tear along the fold because it is on grain.

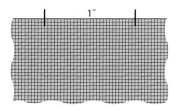

If, however, the fabric is folded on true bias, counting the threads from both directions there are about 140 threads per inch. More threads will need to break before that same size hole appears. And if something catches, a tear is less likely to follow the fold because it is not on grain.

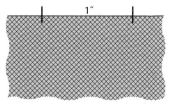

140 threads/inch

If a binding method requires bias, it will be stated. If there is not a mention of it, either straight grain or bias can be used. Your choice.

How Much Fabric Do I Need?

Figure fabric requirements either with the table for a quick, generous yardage or the step-by-step method for an exact amount. The chart is for straight grain strips. Add ⅛ yard more for individually-cut bias strips.

USING THE YARDAGE TABLE
Make note of the width of the binding strip, S, that you need and the finished size of your project, length, L, and width, W.

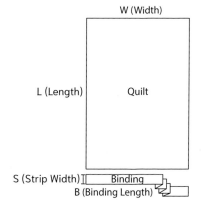

Figure the length of binding, B, required by adding the four sides of the quilt plus 10˝ extra for joining the ends. An example is given for a quilt that is 45˝ × 60˝ and 2½˝ binding width.

B = 2(L + W) + 10

Our example has the length of binding as 2(45 + 60) + 10 = 220.

Yardage Table				
STRIP WIDTH	**LENGTH OF BINDING REQUIRED, B***			
2˝	160˝ (4)	240˝ (6)	440˝ (11)	600˝ (15)
2¼˝	160˝ (4)	200˝ (5)	360˝ (9)	520˝ (13)
2½˝	120 (3)	200˝ (5)	320˝ (8)	480˝ (12)
2¾˝	80˝ (2)	160˝ (4)	280˝ (7)	440˝ (11)
YARDAGE REQUIRED**	⅜ yard	½ yard	¾ yard	1 yard

The number of strips that can be cut from the yardage is in parentheses.
*Yardages have an additional strip width for good measure plus 3˝ to allow for straightening and shrinkage of the fabric.

Find your strip width along the left side of the table. Read across and find the number that is just greater than your project's length of binding. Then along the bottom of the table find the corresponding yardage required. In parentheses is the number of strips that can be cut from this yardage.

For our example, the third row down is 2½˝ and 310˝ in the third column is larger than what we need, 220˝. Therefore, reading at the bottom of the column, we need to buy ¾ yard binding fabric, which yields 8 strips. To get the exact number of strips to cut, divide length of binding by 40 and round up to the next whole number. In this example, 220/40 = 5.5. Rounding up yields 6 strips that need to be cut.

Another way to use this table, is if you know the yardage that is available and the perimeter of the quilt, you can find which width of strip is possible. If you are confident in your cutting abilities, you may be able to get a wider binding because there is an allowance for an extra strip in the amount of fabric listed.

For example, if we have ½ yard of fabric and need 200˝ of binding, the only width that will work is 2˝. Since an extra strip is allowed, with careful cutting 2¼˝ and 2½˝ are also possible.

When cutting individual bias strips, the corner pieces are not used. To allow for this, figure the yardage as with straight grain strips. Then add ⅛ yard more to the amount to cover the loss of these corners.

FIGURING EXACT YARDAGE

Make note of the width of the binding strip, S, that you need and the finished size of your project, length, L, and width, W.

Figure the length of binding, B, required by adding the four sides of the quilt plus 10˝ extra for joining the ends. Divide by 40˝ and round up. This is the number of strips, N, needed.

$N = [2(L + W) + 10]/40$ (round up)

Example with 45˝ × 60˝ finished quilt with 2½˝ binding strip width:

$N = [2(45 + 60) + 10]/40$ (round up)

Number of strips = 220/40 = 5.5, rounding up yields 6.

To figure yardage, multiply the number of strips by the strip width, S. Add an additional strip width for good measure plus 3˝ to allow for straightening and shrinkage of the fabric. Divide by 36˝ to find the yardage needed. Round up to the nearest ⅛ yard. See the table for conversions. If cutting individual bias strips, add another ⅛ yard to allow for the corner pieces that are not used.

$Yardage = [(N \times S) + S + 3˝]/36˝$

Example:

$Yardage = [(6 \times 2.5˝) + 2.5˝ + 3˝]/36˝ = 20.5/36 = .57$, round up to 0.625 which is ⅝ yard.

Yardage: Convert Fractions to Decimals to Inches							
YARDAGE	⅛ YARD	¼ YARD	⅜ YARD	½ YARD	⅝ YARD	¾ YARD	1 YARD
DECIMAL	0.125 yard	0.25 yard	0.375 yard	0.5 yard	0.625 yard	0.75 yard	1.0 yard
INCHES	4½˝	9˝	13½˝	18˝	22½˝	27˝	36˝
METERS	0.2	0.3	0.4	0.5	0.6	0.7	1.0

Cutting Strips on Straight Grain

Here are some benefits of this cutting method:

- Know before you cut that strip will be straight
- More control with shorter ruler
- No turning mat or walking around cutting area
- Know before hand to straighten fabric

If you are right-handed, work at the left end of the yardage and mat. If you are left-handed, work at the right end of the yardage and mat. Left-handed instructions are in parentheses.

1. For lengthwise grain, make the first fold bringing the selvages together so they are parallel and the fabric lays flat. Holding the fabric by the folds and letting any ripples fall out is a good way to be sure the lengthwise grain is aligned and there are no twists.

Parallel selvages

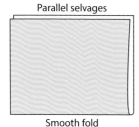

Smooth fold

2. Make the second fold by covering the selvages with the first fold. Now, you see only what needs to be seen. Be sure the second fold is smooth with no lumps or tucks inside. The key to a straight cut is that both the first and second folds are parallel to each other.

3. Align the ruler along the lower fold and check that the top fold runs parallel to a ruler line along the section of fabric to be cut into strips. If the folds are not parallel, see the tip (page 22) for how to reposition the fabric.

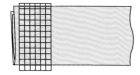

Now that the folds are parallel, with the ruler at the left (right) end of the fabric, rule lines parallel to the top and bottom folds, and the fabric under the ruler just wide enough for one strip and any uneven scrap edge that needs to be trimmed (2″ plus scrap is shown), cut along the right (left) edge of the ruler.

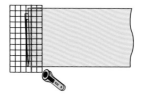

4. Turn this small cut section of fabric around. Align the correct rule line along the cut edge and have the folds parallel to the top and bottom rule lines. Do you see the C shape, along the top fold, down the side, and across the bottom fold? C is for Cut. If you have a C lined up, you can cut knowing the strip will be straight. Continue cutting strips from the remaining folded yardage looking for the C. If the folds and correct width cannot be aligned, refold and trim again by cutting a strip width plus the piece to be trimmed, Steps 2–3.

C is for Cut.

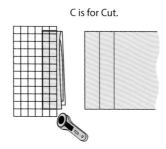

IF FOLDS ARE NOT PARALLEL

Crooked strips happen when one fold is not parallel to the ruler (and the other one is). Under the ruler, the fabric measures one side longer than the other. To make the sides equal, which makes the folds parallel, lift the top fold slightly and shift this fabric toward the longer side, which brings the shorter side up and the longer side down. The diagram shows the extra triangle of fabric which causes crooked strips. Understanding where this comes from and looking for the C when cutting, you will always know before you cut that the strips will be straight!

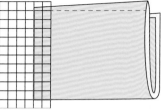

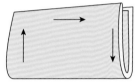

Lift and shift.

Cutting Strips on Bias

Here is how to cut individual bias strips from a square or a rectangle, and how to cut a continuous bias strip. Left-handed instructions are in parentheses.

CUT INDIVIDUAL STRIPS FROM A SQUARE

1. With the square on point, fold along the diagonal, bringing the lower corner up to the upper corner. Fold again bringing the first fold up toward the points.

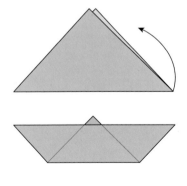

2. Align the ruler along the lower fold and be sure the top fold runs parallel to a ruler line. Check several places across the folded section. Determine where to start cutting at the left (right) end, where the first strip will be about 10˝ or longer. Position the ruler with lines parallel to the top and bottom folds, and cut along the right (left) edge of the ruler. Set aside the smaller piece that is on the left (right).

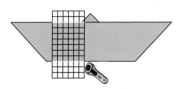

3. Align the correct rule line along the cut edge and have the folds parallel to top and bottom rule lines. Look for the C shape, along the top fold, down the side, and across the bottom fold. Continue cutting strips, looking for the C. If the folds and correct width cannot be aligned, refold and trim again by cutting a strip width plus the piece to be trimmed. See If Folds Are Not Parallel (page 22).

CUTTING EXTRA LONG STRIPS

If the fabric is too wide to fit under the ruler when double folded, most likely there is a larger ruler available. However, if the fabric is really wide, like 108˝ backing fabric, the fabric can be folded one more time with extra care to keep the fabric flat, smooth, and no gaps. As long as all folds are parallel, the strips will be straight.

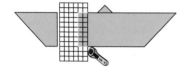

CUT INDIVIDUAL STRIPS FROM A RECTANGLE

1. When working with a rectangle (shown is 18˝ x 40˝, ½ yard), have the fabric open as a single layer and positioned on a diagonal, up toward the right (left). Fold along the diagonal, bringing the lower corner to the upper edge. Fold again bringing the first fold to the point up, so the section to be cut is slightly less than 12˝ high.

2. Align the ruler along the lower fold and make sure the top fold is parallel to a rule line. Check several places across the folded section. Determine where to start cutting at the left (right) end, where the first strip will be about 10˝ or longer. Position the ruler to the left (right) of this point, with rule lines parallel to the top and bottom folds. Cut along the right (left) edge of the ruler. Set aside the smaller piece that is on the left (right).

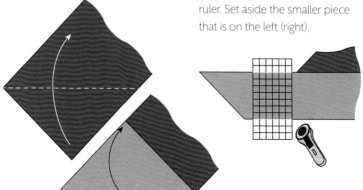

3. Align the correct rule line along the cut edge and have the folds parallel to the top and bottom rule lines. Look for the C shape, along the top fold, down the side, and across the bottom fold. Continue cutting strips, looking for the C. At some point the ruler will not be long enough. Open the fabric and refold. If the folds and correct width cannot be aligned, refold and trim again by cutting a strip width plus the excess to be trimmed. See If Folds Are Not Parallel (page 22).

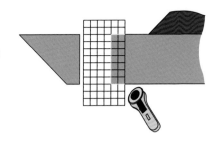

- -

CUT A CONTINUOUS BIAS STRIP

Using a square or rectangle of fabric, bias strips can be cut as one long continuous piece. To begin, use the chart to determine what size of fabric to use.

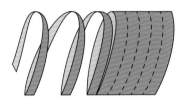

Yield from Yardage for Continuous Bias Binding					
BINDING STRIP WIDTH	**18˝ × 20˝ FAT QUARTER**	**18˝ × 40˝ ½ YARD**	**25˝ × 25˝**	**27˝ × 40˝ ¾ YARD**	**30˝ × 30˝**	**36˝ × 40˝ 1 YARD**
2˝	150˝	280˝	295˝	460˝	430˝	635˝
2¼˝	130˝	250˝	260˝	410˝	380˝	565˝
2½˝	120˝	225˝	235˝	365˝	340˝	510˝
2¾˝	105˝	200˝	210˝	335˝	310˝	460˝

Whether using a square or rectangle, the fabric piece must be square at all four corners. Trim selvages and irregular edges as follows (the yardage does allow for trimming the edges): Fold the fabric with two edges "aligned" as if they were selvages. Double fold if needed and cut the raw ends square to the folds as described on page 21. Refold the piece with the cut ends matching like selvages. Double fold if needed and cut the raw ends in a similar manner.

Since rectangles are more generalized, the illustrations show a rectangle, but the same technique works for fabric squares. Left-handed instructions are in parentheses.

With the rectangle (or square) right side up and horizontal, fold the lower right (left) corner up so that the right (left) edge aligns with the top edge. With a rotary cutter and long ruler or with scissors, cut along the fold. Slide this piece to the left (right).

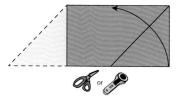

With right sides together, sew the two pieces together, aligning the square corner first. The triangle point will not show like an "ear." Press the seam open. Turn the unit with right side up so that the seam is to the right (left) and the straight grain is along the horizontal edges. On the lower left (right) corner, with a rotary cutter and ruler, cut 8″–10″ of the desired strip width.

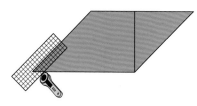

Fold the lower edge up to the upper edge, right sides together, while shifting the lower edge to the left. Leaving the cut portion loose, align the corner of the lower edge to the corner of the upper edge. Make the "ear" at this intersection match the size of your seam allowance. Pin parallel to this seam because there is a twisting of the fabric. Sew and press the seam open. Turn the tube right side out to make the next step easier.

From where the beginning of the strip was cut, continue to cut the strip the appropriate width. For smaller yardage, cutting with scissors is best. Make a strip of fabric or paper the desired width and place it on top of the fabric as a guide for cutting. For larger yardage, placing a mat inside the tube and cutting with rotary cutter and ruler makes for quick work.

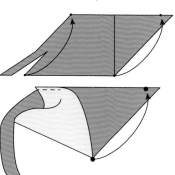

Joining Strips Together

To get one long binding strip, sew individual strips together. Diagonal seams are less obvious and when pressed open they reduce bulk.

When two strips are overlapped, a key point is the point where one strip's edge crosses the other strip's edge. The example shows four key points.

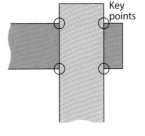

To make one long strip from these two, no matter how they are crossed, sew from one key point to the key point that is diagonally opposite; keep the two long ends on one side of the seam and the two short ends on the other side of the seam.

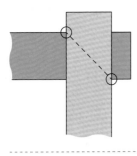

Standard 90° angle

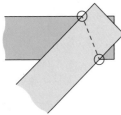

Angle less than 90°, good when short of fabric

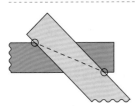

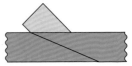

Angle greater than 90°, good to know

Open the seam to be sure the two strips are continuous and straight. Trim the seam allowance to ¼". Press the seam open to reduce the bulk.

Crooked or Staggered Strips?

If the pressed strips are skewed and staggered, then one key point was missed. Sew the correct line from key point to key point. Then remove original stitches.

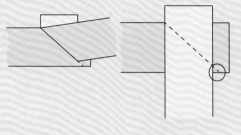

If the pressed strips are only staggered, then both points were missed an equal amount. Sew the correct line from key point to key point. Then remove the original stitches. To avoid this, pin the strips together, mark the line, and then sew.

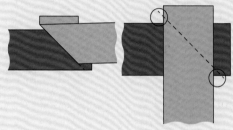

If one strip is sewn to the shorter end of the other strip, the wrong key points are sewn. Sew the correct line between the other two key points and then remove the original stitches.

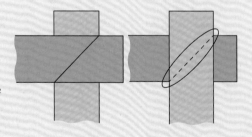

If the pressed strips are only skewed, then the strips are different widths. Remove original stitches and replace the incorrect strip.

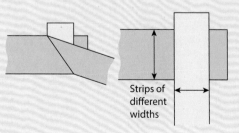

Strips of different widths

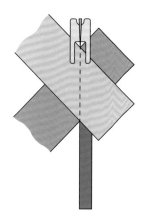

GET IT STRAIGHT To sew these seams easily without marking, have a marked line on the bed of the machine that is a straight line from the needle at the center position out to the front edge of the machine. Such a line may already be on your machine bed. If not, it can be made with a piece of painter's tape or a specialized quilting tool that attaches to the bed of the machine. Once the line is marked, position one key point at the needle, and then sew with the other key point following along the line.

Pressing

Many of the techniques have steps requiring pressing. If working with cotton batting, set the temperature to the cotton setting. However, when using polyester batting, the iron needs to be at a lower temperature so the batting does not melt.

When working with cotton fabrics, especially strips cut on the bias, have a piece of flannel fabric on the ironing board. The cotton fabric will "stick" to the flannel and the iron will not stretch the fabric. However, do not use this when pressing large pieces of cotton fabric as the pieces will drag on the flannel.

For double fold binding, do **not** press the binding strip in half before applying it to the quilt. Once the fabric is rolled around to the other side, more fabric is on the outside than on the inside, so the fold is not at the halfway point. If you must press, do not expect the fold to align with the stitch line on the back or to lay flat on the quilt top.

Stitches—Hand and Machine

Several hand knots and stitches are used throughout these techniques. There is not a lot of strain on these stitches, so use a single thread. Select a thread color that matches the binding fabric and is of a slightly darker value so it hides in the shadows.

Tailor's Knot

This knot is great because it ties the thread into the fabric and is not bulky. Take a small stitch where you want the knot to be, leaving a short tail. Take another small stitch just above the previous and pull the thread to make a loop.

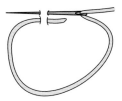

Make a larger loop with the remaining thread, around the small loop. Run the needle into the small loop from top to bottom.

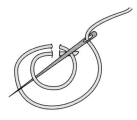

Pull the needle out of the large loop to make a figure 8. Pull slowly so the thread doesn't knot unexpectedly.

Quilter's Knot

Having a consistent size knot gives confidence that the knot will function and, better yet, will not malfunction. The quilter's knot is just such a knot.

Thread the needle. Place the long end of the thread across the needle. While holding the thread end down between your thumb and forefinger wrap the thread closest to the tip of the needle around the needle 3–4 times.

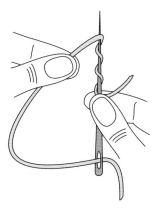

Holding the wrapped thread securely between your thumb and forefinger, pull the needle up until the length of thread has slipped through your fingers, leaving a consistent-sized knot at the end.

Blind Stitch

This stitch can be close to invisible. It is also called the appliqué stitch. Basically, it is a simple, single stitch that runs under one layer and catches just a small bite of the upper layer. Then the stitch is repeated beginning directly below where the thread comes out. Begin and end with a tailor's knot, or quilter's knot, hidden where possible.

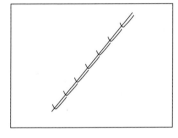

Whipstitch

Take parallel stitches across the section to be whipped together. Begin and end with a tailor's knot or quilter's knot, hidden where possible.

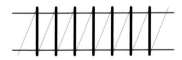

Tack for Mitered Corners

Use a wide machine zigzag stitch, 4.0–6.0 with a 0.0–0.5 stitch length. Stitch across the miter to hold the edges down. For a cleaner finish, either sew a couple of 0 length, 0 width stitches or leave long threads to tie and clip.

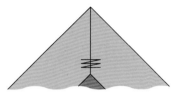

Blind Hem Stitch

This stitch is used for attaching tatting to a binding, or can be used for hemming. Similar to the blind stitch for hand work, a small stitch is taken from one fabric and the main stitch happens on the lower fabric. Check the settings that work best on your machine. Here is what it looks like stitched.

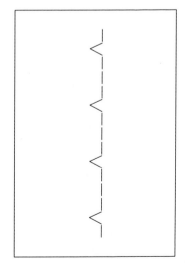

SIMPLE FINISHES

You can finish a project without using additional binding fabric. These tried-and-true techniques can complete your quilt in a pinch, make your project easier, or can be the best way to finish your piece. Knowing the following techniques will give you more options when it comes to finishing your sewing projects.

Self-Binding

Self-binding uses the backing fabric as the binding. The backing is folded in on itself and then folded at the edge of the batting onto the top. Then it is stitched down by machine. There are two ways to trim the batting, either at the edge of the quilt top or extended beyond the quilt top. And there are two ways to fold the corner, either overlapped or mitered. Quilting should stop at the ¼″ seam allowance around the edges of the quilt in all cases.

TRIMMING

If the batting is trimmed at the edge of the quilt top, the self-binding overlaps the quilt top by ½˝ or so and has the appearance of a traditional binding. If the quilt is pieced to the edge, this method cuts off pieced points. With the batting extended out beyond the top, the backing can be folded so that it covers right at the seam line preserving the piecework (as shown in the photo on page 31). Also, if it is wide enough, this finish can look like another border.

At the Edge

Using scissors, trim the batting to align with the edge of the quilt top. Be careful to not cut the backing! At each corner, on the diagonal, snip off about ⅛˝ of the batting.

Measuring from the edge of the quilt top, trim the backing fabric to two times the finished width of the desired binding plus ⅛˝ to allow for the batting. For our example, the finished width is ½˝. This would be 2 × ½˝ = 1˝. Plus ⅛˝ = 1⅛˝.

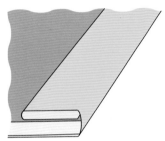

Extended

When trimming the batting and backing, measure from the seam allowance rather than the edge of the quilt top. (In this case, the seam allowance is where you want the edge of the binding to be as it overlaps the quilt top.)

With a cutting mat placed between the batting and backing, use a ruler and rotary cutter to trim the batting to the binding's finished size from the quilt top seam allowance. At each corner, on the diagonal, snip off about ⅛˝ of the batting.

Trim the backing at 3 times the finished size plus ⅛˝, from the quilt top seam allowance. For our example, 3 × 1˝ = 3˝. Plus ⅛˝ = 3⅛˝.

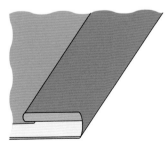

FOLDING CORNERS

The two methods, overlapped or mitered, can be used for either trimming at the edge or the extended batting. Illustrations show both types. The first two steps are the same for both types, so start here.

1. Fold in each side of the backing about an ⅛″ away from the edge of the quilt and press. Avoid pressing the first fold flat.

2. Unfold the backing. Following the diagonal line from the fold point on the edge of one side to the fold point on the edge of the other side, trim the fabric, cutting off the corner. Caution: This is not at the batting!

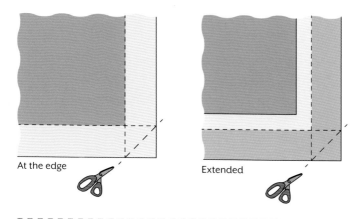

At the edge   Extended

Overlapped

These steps follow steps 1 and 2 in Folding Corners, above.

3. Fold in one side halfway, with the edge of the backing about ⅛″ from the edge of the quilt and batting. Press. Repeat this fold on the adjacent side. Note which side was pressed in first. See pressing tips (page 28).

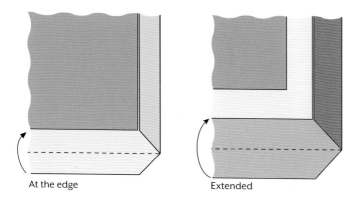

At the edge   Extended

4. Again fold in the first side at the edge of the quilt, covering the quilt top by the desired width. Then fold the other side. By alternating the folds, there are fewer layers to stitch closed.

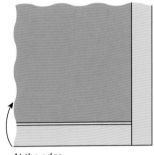

At the edge

Extended

5. Stitch the folds down by hand with a blind stitch (page 30). Or stitch the folds down by machine with a straight or decorative stitch, or by hand with an Embroidery Stitch (page 37). At the corners use a whipstitch to close the folded ends.

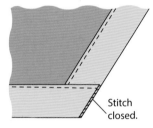

Stitch closed.

Mitered

These steps follow steps 1 and 2 in Folding Corners, page 33.

3. Fold the diagonal edge of the backing in so that the fold lines meet the batting edges. For the extended trim, the center of the diagonal fold should be ¼˝ over the corner of the quilt top. Press.

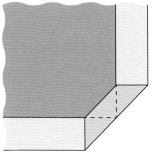

At the edge

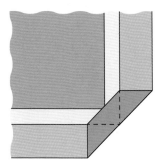

Extended

4. Fold each side in halfway so the edge of the backing meets the edge of the batting. The end points of these folds align with the fold points from before. Press.

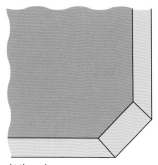

At the edge

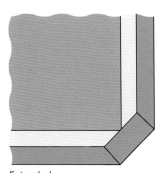

Extended

5. Fold in again at the original pressing at the batting edge. The ends of these folds come together to make the miter. Adjust as needed following the tip below. Press.

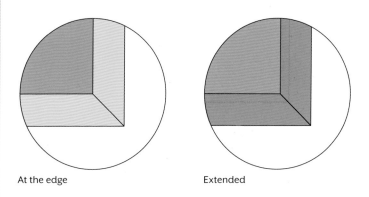

At the edge   Extended

6. Stitch the folds down, by machine with a straight or decorative stitch, or by hand with an Embroidery Stitch (page 37). Stitch the miters down by hand with a blind stitch (page 30).

NEEDING ADJUSTMENTS? If your mitered corner is not looking right, here are some trouble-shooting tips.

If the inner points do not meet, the angle is not kept true on the first diagonal fold.	If the corner has a gap, too much fabric is folded in on the diagonal.	If the corner is overlapped, too little fabric is folded in on the diagonal.
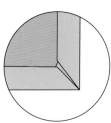	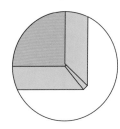	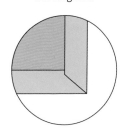

Embroidery Stitch on Front

For self-binding or when binding is applied to the back and rolled to the front, a hand-embroidery stitch can be used to secure the binding. The stitches are made on the top of the binding through the batting and do not go through to the back of the quilt.

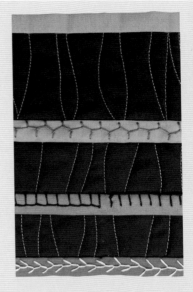

Use embroidery floss or thin perle cotton, size 12 or so, and a needle with a large eye and sharp point. Select a stitch with a simple design that covers a distance easily. At right are three examples. To begin and end a length of thread, use a tailor's knot (page 29) in the seam allowance. Travel from the knot to the front through the binding fabric. To sew these stitches, bring the needle up at the solid green circle, allow the thread to loop as shown, and take a stitch from the pink circle along the dashed line to the green circle. Pull slightly in the direction of the stitch to straighten the thread. Repeat the process, from the green circle, looping the thread, and taking a stitch.

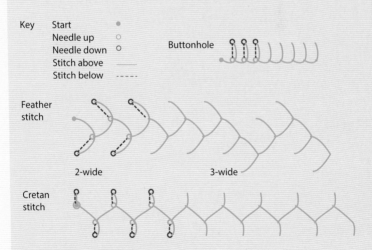

Key
Start •
Needle up ○
Needle down ○
Stitch above ⎯⎯⎯
Stitch below - - - - -

Buttonhole

Feather stitch

2-wide   3-wide

Cretan stitch

On the last stitch, bring the needle out between the binding and the top. Under the fold, make a tailor's knot. Pull the needle and thread through the binding and trim the tail close to the binding.

Turned (Pillowcase or Envelope)

This technique is sewing quilt top and backing right sides together, with the batting in place, before any quilting is done. An opening is left in the seam, the piece is turned right side out, and the opening stitched shut. Then the project is quilted. There are two variations here. One is for lightweight, fluffy battings, with the batting stitched into the seam. The other is for dense battings, with the batting not in the seam.

Front

Back

Layer the quilt top wrong side down on the batting. Smooth so they are flat. Using a rotary cutter, ruler, and mat, trim the batting to the edge of the quilt top. Place the top and batting sandwich right sides together with the untrimmed backing fabric. Pin in place as needed depending on the size of the piece.

Right sides together

Choose a section along one side away from the corners that will be left open for turning the project. This needs to be large enough to push the entire project through; a minimum of 5˝ and maybe even more than 12˝. At one end of this section, backstitch and begin sewing at ¼˝ in from the edge of the batting (which is the upper layer) and the quilt top through all three layers.

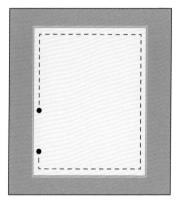

Sew each side pivoting at the corners. Stop sewing the desired distance from the beginning stitching. See "A Turning Point" (page 41) for tips on neat corners.

To give a nice straight edge, separate the front and back seam allowances and press the backing seam allowance back towards itself. At the opening, fold the front seam allowance over the batting and press. Then fold the backing seam allowance over the batting and press.

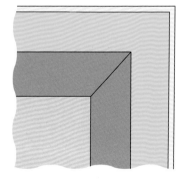

If desired, trim excess batting from the seam allowance with scissors. Be careful to cut only the batting.

With a rotary cutter, ruler, and mat, trim the backing fabric to the edge of the quilt top. Trim each corner.

Turn the piece right side out. Straighten the edges and press where needed. Hand stitch the opening closed with a blind stitch (page 30). Or machine stitch with a straight stitch or decorative stitch all the way around catching the opening so it is closed.

A TURNING POINT When sewing the corner, use shorter stitches , 1.8 mm or 14 spi, about 1˝ before and after the corners. At each corner, stop needle down just before the pivot point where the seam lines cross, and pivot halfway. Take 2–3 stitches diagonally across the corner. Stop needle down, pivot the rest of the way. Continue stitching, changing the stitch length back to the longer length.

these in place and push the tip of this folded section into the back fabric while pulling the back fabric over the tip.

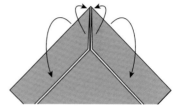

Once this is turned, a little bit of manipulation should have the point looking good. If it is bulky, hammer it flat using a standard hammer on a solid surface with the point between layers of fabric. This is used by tailors to reduce the bulk at intersecting seams, points of collars, corners on cuffs, etc.

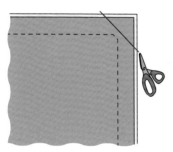

Trim on the diagonal, but not too close. Knowing how much to trim will come with experience. Also, how close you can get depends on the fabric being used.

To turn the point, fold down each side of the trimmed seam allowance toward each other like a miter. Hold

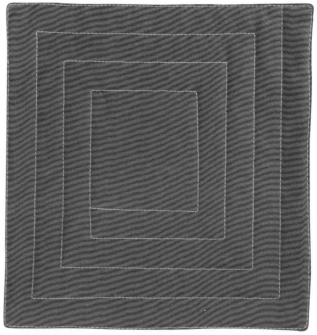

Front

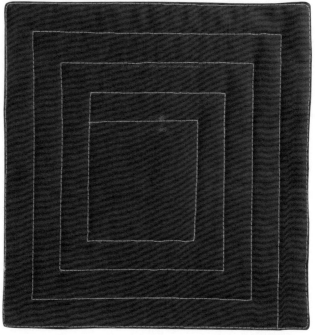

Back

First, square up the quilt top. Then cut the batting slightly smaller than the top as follows:

Place the quilt top on top of the uncut piece of batting so that the top is close to the upper right corner. Trim the batting along the quilt top edge on two adjacent sides.

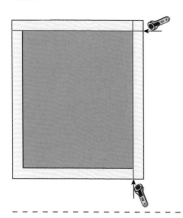

Flip the two layers over and shift the batting so the top extends beyond the batting by ⅝″ on the trimmed sides.

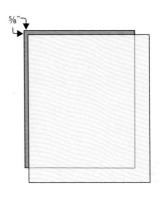

Keeping the layers together, flip them over again and trim along the other two adjacent sides of the quilt top.

Now center the batting on the wrong side of the top. From the **batting side**, baste the top and batting together with large stitches about every 1″–3″ along the edges, about 1″ in from the edge. If it is a larger piece, also baste in the center about every 6″. If safety pins are the preferred method for basting, pin from the quilt top side.

With backing slightly larger than the top, place the quilt top right sides together with the backing. The batting is on top but will not be stitched through. If needed, pin baste the layers together in a few places around the edges, especially at the corners.

Choose a section along one side that will be left open for turning the project. This needs to be large enough to push the entire project through; a minimum of 5″ and maybe even more than 12″. At one end of this section, with the batting on top, backstitch and begin sewing at ¼″ in from the edge of the quilt top next to the batting through the quilt top and backing fabric only.

Sew each side, pivoting at the corners. Stop sewing and back stitch at the desired distance from the beginning. See A Turning Point (page 41).

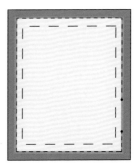

EXTRA STITCHES FOR A PERFECT EDGE

Baste the opening with a 4.0 stitch. Press the seam allowances away from the stitches, the quilt toward the quilt, the back toward the back. Remove the basting so the piece can be turned. The folds will be a guide when stitching the opening closed.

Trim the backing fabric at the edge of the quilt top. Clip the corners on the diagonal, not too close to the stitching.

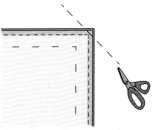

Leave batting basting stitches

Do remove any basting that goes through all three layers. Leave the basting that holds the batting in place.

For a straight finish, from the back, press the backing seam allowance back on itself at the stitch line. Then flip the work over and do the same thing with the quilt top, pressing it back on itself. This pressing gives a straight finish once the piece is right side out.

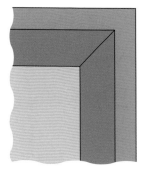

Turn the piece right side out. Smooth out the layers so there are no wrinkles. Align and press edges as needed for a nice, straight edge. Either hand stitch the opening closed or machine stitch close to the edge all the way around the project. Quilt or tie, especially within ½˝ of the quilt edges to catch the batting. Remove the basting as the layers are stabilized.

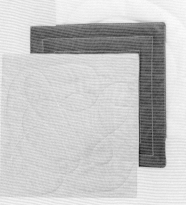

Turned? Pillowcase? Knife-Edge? Envelope?

The terms turned, pillowcase, and envelope all refer to the same process: sewing quilt top and backing right sides together, turning, and then quilting the layers together.

Knife-edge refers to stitching the edge **after** quilting. The batting is not in the seam allowance making for a thin finish.

Knife-Edge

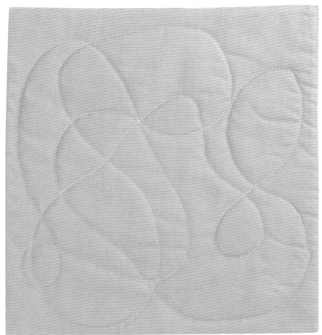

Front

Back

A knife-edge finish is done after the layers are quilted together. Both the quilt top and the backing will be turned in so that the quilt design goes all the way to the edge without the visual interruption of a binding. This is best used with quilt tops and backs that are minimally pieced at the edge.

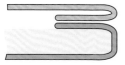

For the knife-edge finish, the batting is trimmed ¼″ less than the top and quilting can not extend beyond ¾″ in from the edge. Mark a line either with a hand or machine basting stitch or with a removable marking tool. If the quilt will be quilted by someone else, let them know that it is not to be quilted beyond this line. The basting will be removed later.

Once the layers are quilted, trim the backing and the batting to the edge of the quilt top. Working one side of the quilt at a time, fold back the top and the backing and pin in place, exposing the batting. With rotary cutter, ruler, and mat, trim ¼″ more from the batting. Be very careful to not cut the front or back fabrics. The straight line from using the rotary cutter creates a straight finish.

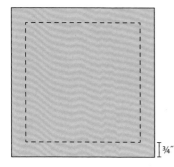

Unpin the top and backing. With the top pulled out of the way, fold and press the backing over the batting. Use a tool such as an awl or seam ripper to hold down corners when pressing.

Fold and press the top over the backing and batting. Now fold in the top so that the crease matches with the backing's crease.

With a blind stitch (page 30), hand stitch the top and backing together or machine stitch very close to the edge, less than ⅛". Remove the basting along the edges.

BINDING FINISHES

The most common way to finish the edge of a layered sewing project is to apply binding, which is a separate strip of fabric. Double fold binding, which is also called French binding, is the most durable, desirable, and easily achieved method. A strip of fabric is folded in half, stitched to the quilt edge, rolled to the other side over the edge, and stitched down. All the others in this chapter are variations of double fold: single fold, striped, pieced, wide, miniature, artist, curved, matched, pieced corner, scallops, and facing. Because everything is based on double fold binding, I will describe that one first, and then each of the others in turn.

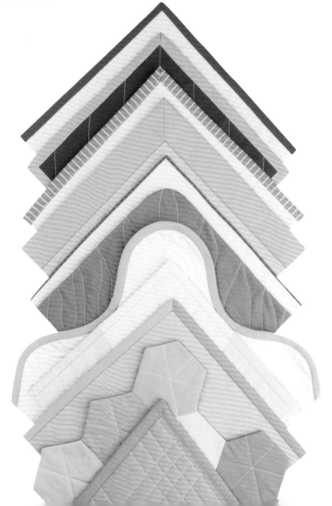

Go-To Basic Double Fold Binding

Double fold binding can be finished by hand or by machine. Because the techniques are similar, I'm giving a single set of instructions with notes for when they are different. The sample instructions are for ⅜″ hand-finished binding or for ⅜″ machine-finished binding.

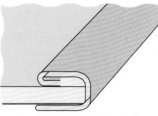

Hand finished double fold binding

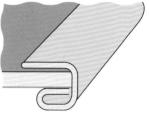

Machine finished double fold binding

Hand finished binding is applied on the front side of the quilt by machine, aligning the edge of the strip with the edge of the quilt top. The strip is rolled to the back and hand stitched over the stitch line.

Machine finished binding is machine stitched to the back, aligning the edge of the strip with the edge of the backing. When the strip is rolled to the front and the fold is machine sewn in place with a topstitch, the stitching shows on the back of the quilt, just inside the binding.

Endless Options: How to Determine Binding Strip Width

To figure the width of the strip (S), it helps to look at a cross section of the binding on the quilt. There is the seam allowance (SA) plus the front finished width (F), the back finished width (B), and an amount for the thickness of the batting (T). Because it is double fold, add these together and multiply this by 2. (Note: When the seam allowance is ¼˝ at the edge of the quilt, add an extra ⅛˝ to allow for the seam that is most often a generous quarter inch.)

$$S = 2 (SA + F + B + T + ⅛˝*)$$

*⅛˝ added if SA = ¼˝.

Here are some common strip widths that you can adjust to meet the needs of the quilt, the fabric, the batting, and your preferences:

¼˝, hand-finished: S = 2 (¼˝ + ¼˝ + ¼˝ + ⅛˝ + *⅛˝) = 2˝

*⅛˝ added if SA = ¼˝.

⅜˝, hand-finished, seam allowance aligned with quilt top, batting trimmed ⅛˝ beyond: S = 2 (¼˝ + ⅜˝ + ⅜˝ + ⅛˝) = 2¼˝ (Note that this size will be used for the Go To hand-finished binding.)

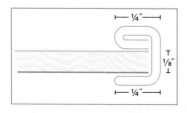

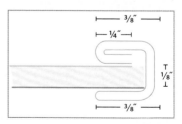

⅜″, hand-finished, with ⅜″ seam allowance: S = 2 (⅜″ + ⅜″ + ⅜″ + ⅛″) = 2½″

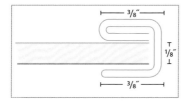

⅜″, machine-finished, ¼″ on back: S = 2 (¼″ + ⅜″ + ¼″ + ⅛″ + *⅛″) = 2¼″ (Note that this size will be used for the Go To machine-finished binding.)

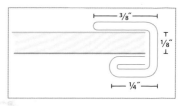

½″, machine-finished, ⅜″ on back: S = 2 (⅜″ + ½″ + ⅜″ + ⅛″) = 2¾″

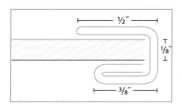

For bindings with seam allowances greater than ¼″, pieced points at the edge of the quilt will be covered by the binding. For methods that do not cover edge points, see Wide Binding (page 70).

Using the length, L, and width, W, of your project, figure the minimum required length of binding: 2 (L + W) + 10″. Figure the yardage required following the instructions on page 18.

GET EVERYTHING READY

Review the tips for setting up your machine (page 16).

This example allows for a low to mid-level loft batting and 2¼″ binding strips, cut either cross-grain or bias.

Using the length, L, and width, W, of your quilt, figure the minimum required length of binding, 2 (L + W) + 10″. From the chart, select the yardage required for the number of 2¼″ cross-grain strips or an equivalent length of bias strips. If you use another size strip, see the crosswise grain and bias tables (pages 19, 24).

Yardage Required by Binding Length				
	⅜ YARD*	½ YARD	¾ YARD	1 YARD
2¼″ BINDING	111″ (3)	185″ (5)	333″ (9)	481″ (13)

*If using individual bias strips, purchase a minimum of ½ yard to have longer strips.

Either cut the strips and join them into one long strip (page 26) or make continuous bias binding (page 24).

If the quilting does not go all the way to the edge, baste all three layers together just inside the edge of the quilt top.

For hand-finished binding, trim the batting and backing ⅛″ beyond the quilt top. For machine-finished binding, trim the batting and backing even with the edge of the quilt top.

Fold the binding strip in half, wrong sides together, as you apply it to the quilt. Do **not** pre-press the binding strip in half with an iron. More fabric is needed on the outside than the inside of the binding, therefore a pressed crease in the middle does not fall where needed.

APPLY THE BINDING

Start close to one corner of the quilt, checking that there will not be a binding seam landing at the next corner. The beginning can be on any side because the join at the end will look like all the others. To find out where to start so seams do not end up at the corners, place the first join/seam in the binding strip 3″–4″ after a corner. Then work back to where the initial strip end needs to be. Leave the first 10″ of binding loose for joining ends later.

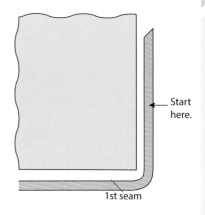

Start here.

1st seam

SEAM AT THE CORNER? If a seam is going to land on a corner, cut it out by cutting the strip 4″–5″ or so before the corner. Cut off the seam and join the rest of the binding. That way the seam is before the corner.

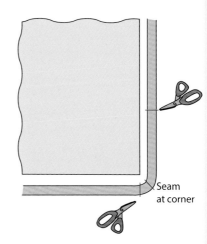

Seam at corner

For a hand-stitched finish, align the raw edges of the binding with the raw edge of the quilt top. Using a ¼˝ seam allowance and beginning the seam with backstitching (or stitching onto the quilt from the side), sew the binding to the quilt through all layers. Continue folding the binding strip in half while sewing. If working with crosswise grain strips, pull slightly on the bottom layer of the binding. This will prevent gathering and tucks on the top layer.

For a machine-stitched finish, on the back of the quilt, align the raw edges of the binding with the raw edge of the backing. Use a generous ¼˝ seam allowance. Sew the binding to the quilt through all three layers. If working with crosswise grain strips, pull slightly on the bottom layer of the binding strip to prevent folds and puckers in the top layer of the binding strip.

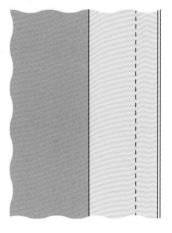

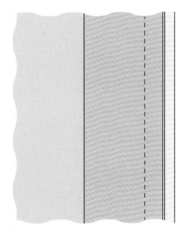

MITER THE CORNERS

A few inches before a corner, stop and mark the pivot point where the two binding seam lines will cross, pushing a pin into the quilt top only so it is perpendicular to the right side. Continue stitching toward the corner. To

prevent a tuck in the corner, stop a stitch before the pivot point, with the needle down. Lift the presser foot, pivot toward the corner, and lower the presser foot. As you sew diagonally to the corner, stay to the right side of the line from the pivot point to the corner. Remove the quilt from the sewing machine.

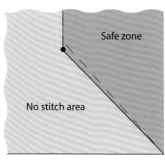

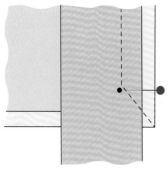

First step to miter a corner of hand-finished binding

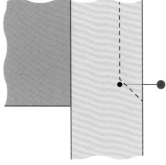

First step to miter a corner of machine-finished binding

Rotate the quilt to work on the next side. While continuing to fold the binding strip in half, fold the binding up along the stitching and adjust the fold to make a straight line from the binding raw edge to the edge of the quilt top on the front or to the edge of the backing on the back. Do not angle the binding to either side.

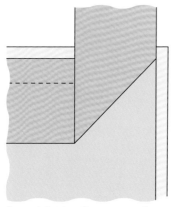

Second step to miter a corner of hand-finished binding

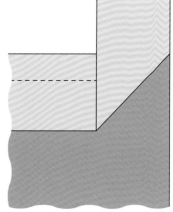

Second step to miter a corner of machine-finished binding

Fold the binding down, with the fold square to the batting and backing. The distance from the seam allowance just sewn (shown horizontally) to the fold should be the finished width of the binding. Be sure you can see the binding underneath at the left and that it does not stick out. Refer to Mitered Corners Exposed (page 61) and Becky's Beauti-Full Binding (page 62) for more information on where this fold needs to be.

Sew from the fold down using the same seam allowance, ¼˝ in from the quilt top on the front, or a generous ¼˝ from the edge on the back. No backstitch is necessary.

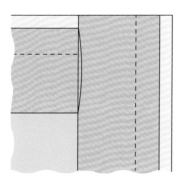

Third step to miter a corner of hand-finished binding

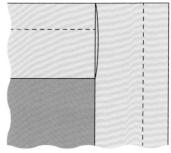

Third step to miter a corner of machine-finished binding

Continue stitching along the sides and mitering each corner, stopping about 10″ from the starting point. Backstitch or stitch off to the side and remove the quilt from the sewing machine.

JOIN THE ENDS

There are many ways to join the ends of the binding with most having common pitfalls. My "twist and shout" method (so named because we twist the strips and shout "It works!") is different in that it is practically foolproof. These are the benefits:

> You always sew the right sides together and in the right direction.

> You know the binding fits before cutting the ends.

> The method uses no tools and works for all sizes of binding.

> They can be joined with less fabric.

To make this easy, leave a space of about 4 times the width of the strip not sewn and where the ends can join in the middle. With both ends of the binding open, place the strips right sides together. Working on a flat surface, have them meet halfway so they lay flat on the quilt. Align the binding edge with the edge of the quilt. Once the strips are positioned, put a slight amount of tension where they join, making the strips taut. The binding should be neither so tight that it pulls the quilt together, nor so slack that the binding can be lifted away from the quilt.

The critical point (CP) for this method is where the strip ends meet on the seam line on the surface of the quilt. Keeping the tension on the strips, pin the strips together at this point, catching only 2–3 threads of each strip.

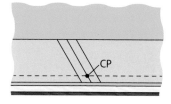

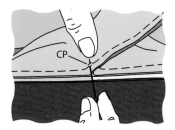

SAFETY PIN METHOD

If catching 2–3 threads with a straight pin doesn't work for you, find the critical point and put a safety pin through it. Then lay the ends flat and realign the critical point. Pin the layers together, stabilizing the CP, and pin the point by catching only 2–3 threads.

At this unfinished section, gather up the quilt and pin it together. Rotate one strip with respect to the other around the critical point. When they are at a sufficient angle to each other that the strips can be laid flat, pin the strips together for sewing. This does not have to be at a 90-degree angle, see Joining Strips Together, page 26.

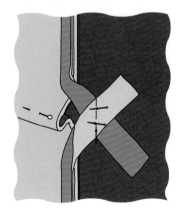

Sew from one point where the strips' edges cross to the opposite point where the strips' edges cross, through the critical point in a straight line. When sewn through the critical point, there is only one possible way to sew this seam.

Fold the binding in half and check the fit. Unfold the strip, trim the seam allowance, and press the seam open. Fold the strip in half and stitch the remaining binding length to the quilt. You've twisted, now you can shout, "It works!"

IF THE STRIP DOESN'T FIT

When you are checking the fit, if there is too much fabric, either the ends were not held down with enough tension or they were pinned for too small of a seam allowance. The critical point is on the seam line.

If there is too little fabric so that the binding does not lay flat, then the strips were either pulled too tight or pinned for too large of a seam allowance.

FINISH THE BINDING

Press the binding back toward the seam allowance, as close to the corners as possible. Fold the binding around to the opposite side of the quilt from where it was applied. For hand-finished binding, the fold aligns with or covers the stitching on the back of the quilt. For machine-finished binding, the fold covers the first line of stitching (showing on the front of the quilt) by ⅛" or so. Whether sewing by hand or machine, use clips or pins to hold the binding in place.

For hand stitching, begin with a tailor's knot (page 29) in the seam allowance and then sew down the fold using a blind stitch or appliqué stitch (page 30). At the corners, looking at the back with the corner pointing up, fold in the right side first. Then fold in the left side. This distributes the bulk. If you are left-handed or hold the quilt in a certain way, you will need to pin this fold ahead of time. As each corner is folded and stitched, stitch up the miter (red lines), poke the needle to the front, stitch down the miter (green lines), and poke the needle to the back again. Continue around, hand stitching the binding.

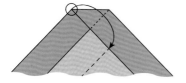

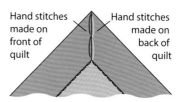

Hand stitches made on front of quilt

Hand stitches made on back of quilt

For machine stitching, sew with a straight or decorative stitch along the fold, through all layers. On the back of the quilt, this stitching will be visible ⅛" or so inside the binding. At the corners, looking at the front with the corner pointing up, fold in the right side first. Then fold in the left side. This distributes the bulk. Pin in place. Continue sewing to the corner, pivot, and sew along the next side. To hold the miters in place, sew a tack across each miter using a zigzag stitch with zero stitch length and 3–4mm width, or hand sew as described in the previous hand sewing method.

If something doesn't seem right on the miters, see Mitered Corners Exposed (page 61).

Big Stitch on Back Sometimes we just want to have fun with the finish. Big Stitch does exactly that and it is quick.

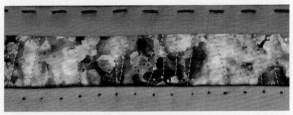

Big stitch (top) and back stitch (bottom)

Depending on the desired result, there are many different kinds of threads that can be used, such as embroidery thread (6 strand) or perle cotton (sizes 8–12). Select the thread and needle that will work for your project. The needle needs to be sharp enough to go through the layers, have a large enough eye to hold the thread, and be able to be pulled through the fabric when threaded. I recommend testing the thread for color fastness.

Use a tailor's knot (page 29) underneath the binding to begin and end the thread lengths. Bring the thread to the top of the binding. Sew the binding to the back and batting using either a running stitch or a small back stitch. For the running stitch, on the left in the illustration below, make even stitches about ⅛˝ to ¼˝ long and even spaces between them. For the small back stitch, on the right in the illustration below, where the needle comes up from the knot, take a small stitch back and bring the needle up about ¼˝ in the direction you are sewing. Take a small stitch back and bring the needle up about ¼˝ away. Continue in this manner. Avoid stitching through to the front of the quilt. Sew close to the fold so the binding is secure.

Mitered Corners Exposed Have you ever bound a quilt and had three corners perfect and the 4th one wonky? Here are the three most common issues and what causes them.

PROBLEM
Corner has a tuck or pucker

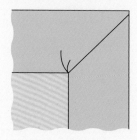

CAUSE
If the corner has a tuck, either the initial stitching was past the pivot point into the no-stitch area (page 55), which is quite common, or when the fold was made the top edge was not parallel, or the lower left edge was tucked under too far. This is fixed by removing stitches and resewing/refolding the corner.

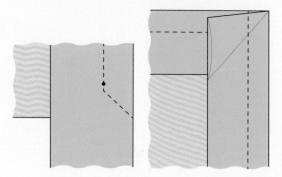

Continued on page 62.

Continued from page 61. ▶

PROBLEM
Rounded Corner

CAUSE
If the corner is rounded, the folded corner is too far down, which is a lesson learned and better next time. Or the binding is folded to the back to align with the stitching and the strip is too wide. To correct this, allow all the fabric to fold to the back extending beyond the stitch line. If you want to make the fold align with the stitching, use a narrower strip width.

← Fold binding snugly to the back.

Becky's Beauti-Full Binding
Becky Goldsmith, author and designer, has developed her own favorite method for a full double fold binding. She uses a 2½˝ strip, trims the batting and backing ¼˝ beyond the top, and aligns the fold for the miter at the quilt edge, not the batting and backing.

PROBLEM
Pointed Corner

CAUSE
If the corner is pointed, the folded corner is too far up or the binding is folded to the back to align with the stitching, but the strip is too narrow.

She trims the batting and backing on the diagonal at the corner. The corner will have a boxed look.

The extra backing and batting provide a structure for the edge of the quilt. It is an example of how to change the measurements for a different, yet successful result.

Single Fold Binding

Highlights:

- Conserves fabric, whether limited amount or for wide binding
- Requires pressing
- Without pressing is challenging to get a straight line

- Only one layer so not as durable

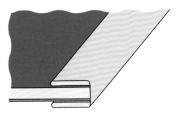

To figure the width of the strip (S), multiply the finished width of binding by 4, which is the same front (F), back, and both seam allowances. Add the thickness of the batting (T).

$S = 4 \times F + T$

For example, with a front and back width of ⅜˝,

$S = 4 \times \frac{3}{8}˝ + \frac{1}{8}˝ = 1\frac{5}{8}˝$

Use the perimeter of your quilt and this number to determine yardage (page 18). Cut the required number of strips. Join them into one long piece for mitered corners.

Fold the strip(s) almost in half with one side offset from the other by ⅛˝. This can be estimated rather than rigidly measured. Press for a crisp line. On the wide side fold the edge close to the center by about ¹⁄₁₆˝ and press.

Follow double fold binding (page 53) with only a single layer, applying the narrow, unfolded side right side down. Join the ends in a similar manner (page 57). Wrap the binding around to the back side with the edge folded under at the pre-pressed line. Hand stitch with a blind stitch.

MACHINE FINISH To machine finish single fold binding, figure the strip width by adding finished front width, F, plus a same size front seam allowance, plus back width, B that is ⅛˝ less, and its matching seam allowance, plus the batting thickness, T.

$$S = 2F + 2B (⅛˝ \text{ less than } F) + T$$

When folding in half, offset by ¼˝ and press. Fold the wider side in toward the center, about ¹⁄₁₆˝ away and press. With the narrow, unfolded edge aligned to the edge of the back of the quilt, stitch and wrap to the front. Stitch the fold in place.

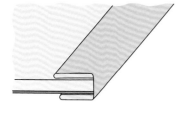

Striped Binding

Using the print of a fabric to add a special look to the binding can be fun. There are three possible effects with stripes: short bursts of color, long lines of color along the edges, and barber pole or candy cane style. Use a plaid for an even more intricate effect.

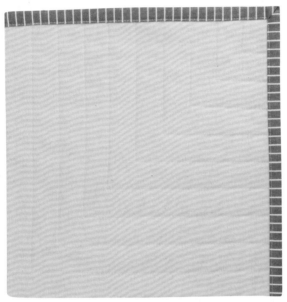

Short stripe

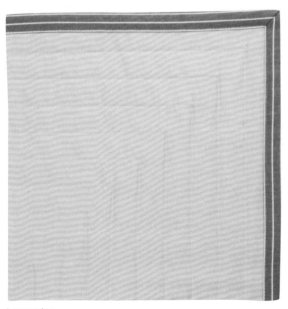

Long stripe

Diagonal stripe

Diagonal Plaid

Select either single fold or double fold binding and the desired look. Determine the yardage based on the necessary grain (page 17). Cut the strips aligning with the print, which may not be the same as the grain. Remember with cutting, all that matters besides strip width is that folds are parallel to each other and appropriately oriented to the desired design. Apply the binding with the chosen method.

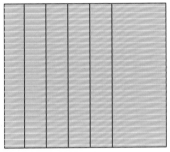

Short stripe: Cut crosswise.

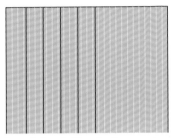

Long Stripe: Cut lengthwise.

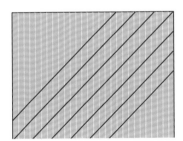

Diagonal stripe: Cut diagonally.

Plaid: Cut diagonally.

Pieced Binding

The perfect binding in some cases may be made with multiple fabrics from the quilt. These can be cut into strips, sewn together into a "striped" fabric, and then cut as mentioned for either the short stripe or the diagonal stripe (stagger strips by the angle of the cut and width of the strips). Alternatively, the binding can be pieced from longer lengths to match the quilt. Or for a scrappy quilt, use the leftover binding strips from other projects.

With each of these methods, keep in mind to use a smaller stitch, 1.5 or so, for the piecing so the stitches are less likely to loosen when applying and manipulating the binding strip. Also, be sure to press all seams open so that there is less bulk at the seams.

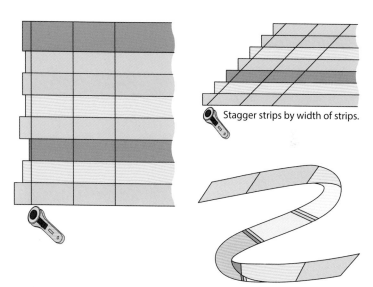

Stagger strips by width of strips.

Wide Binding

Varying the width of the binding can add a frame for the main design. The finish can cover up a wide border or be an extension of the backing and batting allowing pieced points to show. The front and back can be different widths allowing for the back binding to be a design element too.

Here is how to achieve the different looks, knowing the seam allowance (SA), the width of the front (F), the width of the back (B), and an amount for the thickness of the batting (T). This is multiplied times 2 for the finished strip width (S). The general formula is S = 2 (SA + F + B + T)

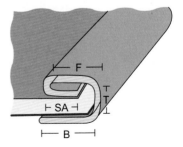

If the binding covers the quilt top, trim the backing and batting to the edge of the quilt top. Apply the binding to the front with a seam allowance the finished width of the binding and the same size finished width on the back. Add ⅛″ for the batting thickness times 2. In this case, SA = F = B, so

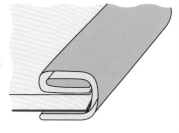

S = 6 F + 2 T

If the binding is to extend beyond the quilt top, trim the batting and backing the front width, F, from the seam line.

If the front is wider than the back, apply the binding to the back, with a seam allowance that is the width of the back.

S = 2 (F + 2B + T)

If the back is wider than the front, apply it to the front, with a ¼″ seam allowance.

S = 2 (¼″ + F + B + T)

For example, for a ¾″ binding on the front and ⅜″ binding applied on the back with a ⅜″ seam allowance and ⅛″ for batting, the size to cut the binding strips is:

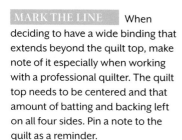

S = 2 (⅜″ + ¾″ + ⅜″ + ⅛″) = 2 (1⅝″) = 3¼″ wide

Apply as in double fold mitered binding following the front or back application (page 51).

- -

MARK THE LINE When deciding to have a wide binding that extends beyond the quilt top, make note of it especially when working with a professional quilter. The quilt top needs to be centered and that amount of batting and backing left on all four sides. Pin a note to the quilt as a reminder.

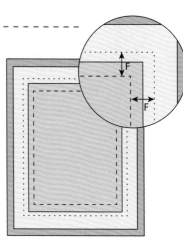

Miniature Binding

These thin bindings are perfect for miniature quilts, wall hangings, and artwork. The ⅛″ is applied as a double fold, and the ¹⁄₁₆″ is a variation on single fold. Each adds a wow factor in their own little way.

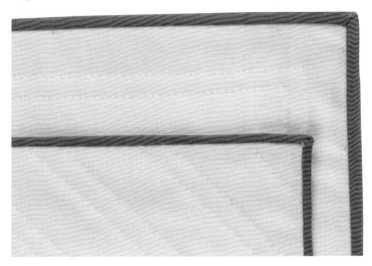

EIGHTH INCH BINDING

This ⅛″ binding is sturdy and can be used on quilts that will get some use. It is applied just like the double fold mitered binding. To achieve this size, the binding is applied with a ¼″ seam allowance which is then trimmed to ⅛″.

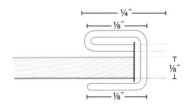

The strip width (S) is figured as follows with the seam allowance (SA), front width (F), back width (B), and thickness for batting (T):

$$S = 2 (SA + F + B + T)$$

$$S = 2 (¼″ + ⅛″ + ⅛″ + ⅛″) = 2 (⅝″) = 1¼″$$

Since the binding is so narrow, a small change in fabric or batting thicknesses can affect the results. Make a sample with this strip width. If needed, adjust to 1⅛″ or 1⅜″ strips. Cut the strips to the desired width. Apply as in double fold mitered binding (page 51) to the front with ¼″ seam allowance and the following differences.

At the corner, one stitch before the pivot point, stitch off at the usual angle. Clip the binding along the diagonal stitching to within ⅛″ of the previous seam.

Now fold the strip down ⅛″ above the previous seam line. Align the binding with the right edge and stitch as before.

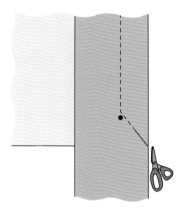

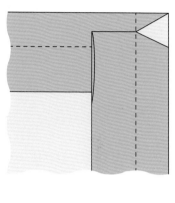

Join the ends like double fold mitered binding (page 57). Trim all layers of the seam allowance to ⅛″ wide; avoid cutting the corner folds. Clip corners on the diagonal.

Roll the binding around to the back and hand stitch with short stitches.

SIXTEENTH INCH BINDING

Sixteenth inch binding is specifically for miniature quilts. To work at this scale the following accommodations should be made.

- Use a smaller needle, 60/8.
- Choose thinner thread, 60 wt or smaller, such as 80 or 100.
- Select high thread count fabric, for example 200 count such as batik.
- Take smaller stitches, about 1.5 or 17 stitches per inch.

Cut the strips at ⅞″ on the bias and join with ¼″ seams trimmed to ⅛″, to the necessary length. Press seams open. Press the strip in half lengthwise.

Apply the binding strip as a single layer to the front of the quilt using a scant ¼″ seam allowance. Miter the corners by stitching off perpendicular to the edge. Fold the strip up, aligning the edge with the next edge. Crease the fabric along the diagonal fold. Unfold the strip and carefully clip along the crease to within ¹⁄₁₆″ of the previous stitching.

Fold the strip down at ¹⁄₁₆″ above the seam and aligned with the right edge. Stitch, beginning at the edge of the quilt with ¼″ seam allowance as before.

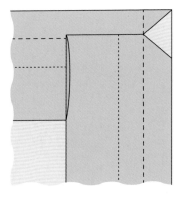

Continue mitering the corners and join the ends like double fold mitered binding (page 53). Trim each edge to ⅟₁₆˝, about 3–4 threads width. At the corners, nip a slight amount of the corner. Stay away from any stitching.

The fold that was pressed in the strip is the fold that will be stitched to the backing. Trim the edge to within ⅟₁₆˝ of the fold. Fold the cut edge into the seam allowance. Roll the binding to the back of the quilt and stitch down the folded edge. Use a blind stitch, ⅟₁₆˝ or so in length, being careful to not catch the front of the quilt.

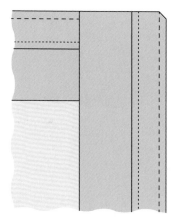

Artist's Binding

Quite often in an art quilt, a binding can take away from the design. Physically, the piece still needs to be bound. One solution is to use a narrow binding and turn everything, including the seam allowance, to the back. This looks similar to the knife edge and is an easier technique.

Select a binding fabric that matches the front or is darker so it appears as a shadow.

Even though this is a straight-line design, bias binding is used because the corners are trimmed very close to the seam lines.

Here is how to figure the width of the strip (S) to cut. The seam allowance (SA) is a standard ¼˝, there is no front, and the back (B) can be any desired width. The second seam allowance, which is folded under, is ⅛˝ less than B. For this example, we are going to finish with a ⅜˝ back.

S = (SA + B + SA) = (¼˝ + ⅜˝ + ¼˝) = ⅞˝ 1˝ binding strips

Use 1˝ because less than that becomes challenging. Know that the finish width will be slightly wider than ⅜˝. Figure the number of strips needed and the yardage required for bias strips (page 18). Cut the bias strips and join together (page 22) or cut continuous bias binding (page 24). Trim the batting and backing to the edge of the quilt top.

Leaving a tail of about 10˝, apply the open strip right sides together to the quilt top with ¼˝ seam allowance. At 1˝ from each corner, shorten the stitch length to 1.5mm (17 spi). Mark the pivot point where the seams cross with a pin sticking out perpendicular. Continue stitching, pivoting just before the point. Stitch off perpendicular.

Fold the strip up, aligning the edge with the next edge. Crease the fabric along the diagonal fold. Unfold the strip and carefully clip along the crease almost to the stitch line.

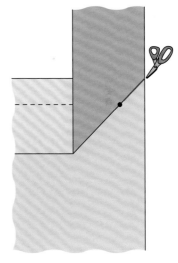

Fold the strip down at the seam and align with the right edge. Be sure you can see the fabric at the left-hand side of the fold. Stitch, beginning at the edge of the quilt, with ¼˝ seam allowance catching the fabric left of the clipped point. Use shorter stitch length as before for about 1˝, then return to regular stitch length.

Continue mitering the corners and stop about 10˝ from the starting point. Join the ends like double fold mitered binding (page 57).

At each corner, about 1˝ on either side, reinforce the stitching using the shorter stitch, and pivoting at the corner point. Carefully trim the seam allowance at this stitching. Undo any quilting stitches in the seam allowances, leaving the threads long. Trim out the batting as close as possible without cutting the front or backing. Grade the seam allowance by trimming the backing to ⅛˝.

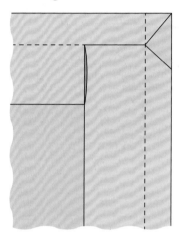

Press the binding toward the seam allowances. With the quilt right side down, fold the binding aligning the raw edge with the trimmed backing and press. Open the fold and staystitch the binding and seam allowance together, between the stitch line and the trimmed backing.

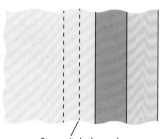

Stay-stitch through seam allowances and binding strip.

Turn the binding and seam allowance to the back while folding under the raw edge. Pin in place so that the binding is visible only on the back. At the corners, fold in one side and overlap the other squared rather than mitered. If there is a lot of bulk, see A Turning Point, page 41. Hand stitch along the folds, taking time at the corners. This can also be machine stitched if a stitch line on the front is desired, though generally it isn't.

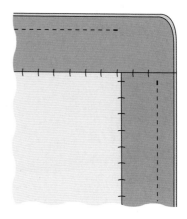

CORNER OPTIONS Getting all of the necessary fabric in the corners is a real challenge. Here are two other options:

CURVED CORNERS
Trim the corners to the desired curve of at least 1˝ in from each side.

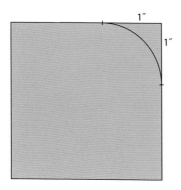

At the rounded corners, sew with a shorter stitch length, 1.5mm (17 spi), and pull the binding slightly on the curve so it will lay flat after it is turned to the back.

TRIMMED CORNERS
Mark lines along both sides of each corner, from 2˝ away from the corner to ⅛˝ in from the side. After marking both lines at the corner, trim along the lines.

The bias strips easily follow the new line, there is more room for the folded binding, and the corner appears square without being pointy.

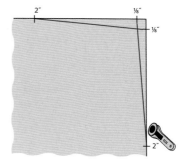

Curved Binding

Every now and then a quilt begs for a curved edge. It could be only at the corners, or a swag all the way around the quilt. The main thing to remember is that the binding must be cut on the bias. This has enough stretch to get around the curves.

Learn the techniques by making the pot holder project (page 134) or just a quick sample of a shoe print shape, about 5˝ × 12˝ in size, for inside (concave) and outside (convex) curves.

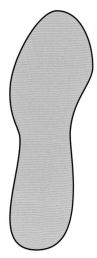

Determine the width of binding to be used. See How Wide Can It Be, below right. Using the perimeter of the quilt, determine the yardage of bias binding required (page 18).

Cut and sew individual bias binding strips (page 22) or make continuous bias binding (page 24).

Apply the binding as usual, either from the front or back depending on the technique being used. There needs to be more fabric on the outside curve and less on the inside curve. When sewing on the outer/convex curves, ease the fabric so that there is more on the left side of the stitching (the fold side). When sewing on the inside/concave curves, stretch the fabric slightly so there is slightly less fabric on the left of the stitching. With practice you will learn just how much is needed for the materials being used, to avoid cupped curves.

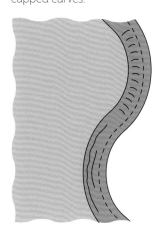

You may find it helpful to pin the binding in place for each curve. When I pin, I pin at the machine, just before sewing each section, as the binding can shift.

WHERE TO ALIGN FOR CURVES

When sewing curves, the fabric should be aligned to a point that is directly to the right of the needle. Looking at the edge of the foot out in front like we are used to doing is not going to give the right curve. If necessary, put a piece of tape with an arrow on it to the right of the foot where everything should align.

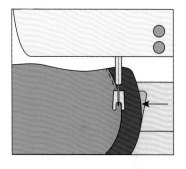

How Wide Can It Be?

There are limitations on how wide a bias binding can be applied to a curve. The maximum that I recommend based on experience is ⅝″ using a 4″ wide binding strip. For this width, the curves cannot be too small. They need to be from a 6″ diameter circle , like a saucer plate, at least. You can use narrower strips on tighter curves. Again, try a sample for what you want to accomplish. Adjust as needed.

Matched Binding

For those who want the benefits of a binding yet want it to virtually disappear, matched binding is one answer. This would be for quilts that are more artistic but still need some wearability to them. Where the design lines change on the quilt, we want them to change at the same angle on the binding.

Determine where the binding fabrics will change. The angle of the design line in the quilt needs to extend straight about five inches into the quilt. If it doesn't, pin a piece of paper over the area and draw a continuation of the line to be used in marking the binding strips. Be careful to not mark on the quilt!

For attaching the binding strips, the more space that can be free on either side of the join, the better. For a 2½˝ binding 10˝ works. Apply sections of binding where desired, leaving the ends open at each change. If a fabric change is close to a corner, pin the corner as if it is being sewn. Then unpin the corner after the critical point between the two fabrics has been found and pinned.

To distinguish the binding from the quilt, we are using four separate colors. Find the critical point that matches the design line as follows: With the fabric strips open, fold each strip back on itself where it meets on the design line at the seam allowance in from the edge—the critical point. Crease the fabrics back on themselves so this perpendicular line is well marked.

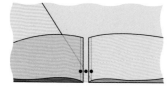

For one strip, align the raw edge with the edge of the quilt, with the critical point in line with the design line. Fold the strip along the seam line toward the quilt edge, with it laying as flat as possible. Mark the design line on the front of the fabric strip using a removable marker. Repeat with the other strip end.

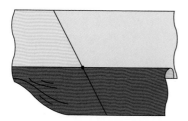

Mark the design line on binding #1

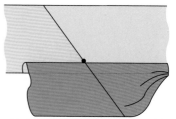

Mark the design line on binding #2

With the strips aligned on the creases, pin them together catching only 2–3 threads, at the critical point where they meet on the seam allowance line. Gather up and pin the quilt so the binding ends can be manipulated. Twist the two fabric ends so they match up on the marked lines.

Baste the seam and check that it works. The stitched seam will appear to be out of alignment by about ½". However, once it is rolled to the back, the seam is in the correct orientation.

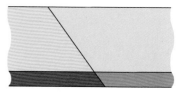

Do not trim the ends until you know that the binding fits and that it lines up with the design lines This may take a few tries to get a great result but it is well worth the effort.

Pieced at the Mitered Corner

Sometimes a quilt needs a little added interest and changing binding fabrics at the corner can be just the ticket.

This technique can be applied with either double fold (more bulk, less folding) or single fold (less bulk, more folding) binding. Decide on the width of the strip to use. Prepare the different strips that will be used for each side.

Apply the first side of binding leaving a tail of 3-4 inches and starting about 2" just after the corner. At the corner, stop one stitch before the seam allowance point. Pivot the work and stitch off square to the edge. Fold the strip up and in line with the next side as usual. Pin in place.

Here is where the change happens. Place the next strip so that the end is above the edge of the quilt and in line with the right side of the quilt. This is as if that strip is being folded down like normal. Pin in place.

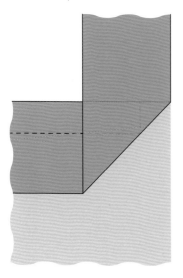

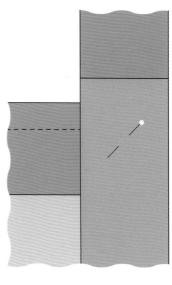

Set the stitch length to 1.0mm (25 spi) and use thin thread, 60–100 wt. From the back side, sew the two strip ends together right at the edge of the quilt. This should be stitched as close as possible. Sew a second line of stitching on top of the first, reinforcing with back stitching at the ends. Trim as close as possible to the stitching, ⅟₁₆˝ or so.

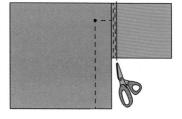

Once binding has been applied to the entire work, fold the binding around to the back. At each corner, snip the corner to trim out excess fabric. Fold the miter with attention to folding in any excess. Hand stitch for more control and great looking miters. If there is still too much bulk at the corner, use a hammer to reduce the thickness (see A Turning Point, page 41).

Facing Binding

Facing is a technique used in garment construction to finish an irregular edge, such as a neckline or collar. A piece of fabric is sewn to the front following along the design line. Then corners are clipped and curves snipped. Once that is done, the binding piece, P, is turned at the edge, covering the entire design, giving a finish that follows the original design. With this method, almost any shape can be easily and neatly finished.

The process is like the Artist's Binding (page 76) in that the binding and its seam allowance are rolled to the back. The difference is that the binding needs to be wide enough to cover the entire design.

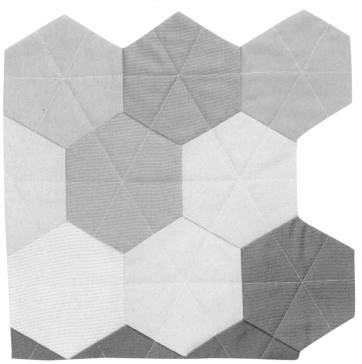

Front

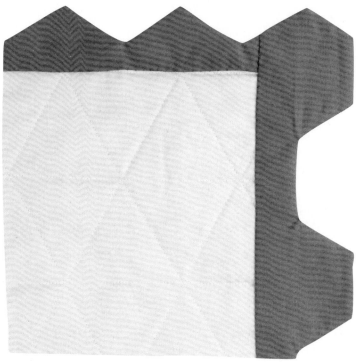

Back

In this sample, notice the difference in the depth of the facing beyond the design lines. The top edge has a minimal amount for a functional finish. The right side has more, to balance out the wider design.

To determine the finished width on the back , B, measure the width of the design from the outer most point of the unfinished edge to the innermost point of the seam line, on a line perpendicular to the width of the design, D. B is this number plus an overlap. Use ⅜″ for a minimal overlap or more for a balanced look.

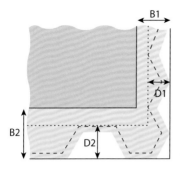

The strip width to cut, for single fold is B + ¼". For double fold, it is 2 times B. As the photo shows, each side of the quilt can be different. For example, if B is 1¾".

For a single fold strip width:

B + ¼"

1¾" + ¼" = 2" wide facing strips

For double fold strip width:

2 B

2 (1¾") = 3½" facing strips

Once the quilt is quilted, using bobbin thread that is a different color than the backing fabric, staystitch following the edge with a scant ¼" seam line. This is your guide for the stitch line as viewed from the back of the quilt.

Cut and sew lengths of facing as needed for each side. Have extra on each end, at least 1½ times the strip width. For single fold, press under ¼" along one edge. For double fold, press the strip in half lengthwise, with wrong sides together. With the facing right sides together with the quilt top, align the raw edge(s) with the outer edges. Pin in place. At the corners, fold the strips back at various points along the seam line to decide how the ends will meet. Most often it is at a miter at the corner. Once decided, mark the folds by pressing and leave the ends loose.

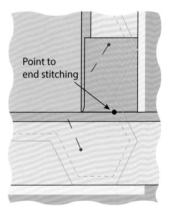

Point to end stitching

Turn the quilt over to the back side and pin through all layers including the facing. Then turn over and remove the pins on the front. Starting and stopping with back stitches where the ends will meet, sew with a 2.0mm or shorter stitch length to the inside (left) of the previous stay stitching.

Cut away excess facing, batting, and backing ¼" outside the stitched seam line (the edge of the quilt top). For a smoother transition, trim out as much batting as possible.

Clip at inside corners and curves, stopping before the stitching. Trim at points.

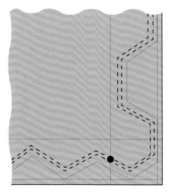

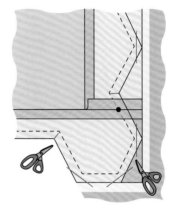

Turn the facing to the back, smoothing out corners, points, and curves. At the end of each strip, verify that the folds meet. Trim at ¼" seam allowance, and pin in place. Hand stitch the folded edge in place and where the ends meet. For a finish that looks like binding, top stitch on the front, ¼" or so away from the edge.

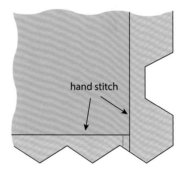

hand stitch

Mitered Corners for Different Angles

Some projects require binding angles other than square corners. Here is how to bind angles wider than 90 degrees (obtuse) and angles narrower than 90 degrees (acute). The strip width and seam allowance can be of any size as with any double fold or single fold binding.

GREATER THAN 90 DEGREES

When applying the binding, before the corner, mark the pivot point where the two seam allowances intersect. Stitch to just before this pivot point, stop with the needle down, turn the quilt, and stitch to the corner staying to the right of the diagonal line, see page 55. Remove the quilt.

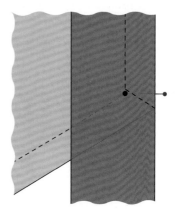

Fold the binding up along the stitching, aligning the raw edge with the next edge.

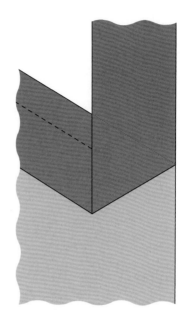

Fold the binding down so that the fold is in line with the outer point of the project. Be sure you can see the fabric at the left hand side of the fold.

Stitch, beginning at the edge, catching the fold.

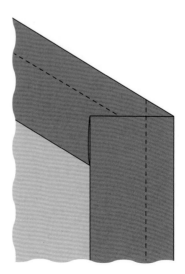

After the binding is attached and it is being turned to the other side, with the corner point up, fold the right side of the corner first.

On the left side, where the binding edge crosses the edge of the quilt, pull that point down and in from the left to make the miter. Depending on the way you hold the quilt when hand finishing, you may need to pre-fold the corners and pin in place.

LESS THAN 90 DEGREES

When applying the binding, before the corner, mark the pivot point where the two seam allowances intersect. Stitch to just before this pivot point, stop with the needle down, turn the quilt, and stitch to the corner staying to the right of the diagonal line. Remove the quilt.

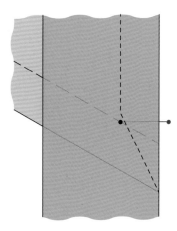

Fold the binding up along the stitching, aligning the raw edge with the next edge.

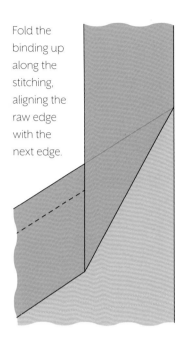

Fold the binding down so that the fold is in line with the outer point of the project. Be sure you can see the fabric at the left hand side of the fold.

Stitch, beginning at the edge, catching the fold. After the binding is attached, at the corners, trim excess fabric in the seam allowance without getting too close to the outer point.

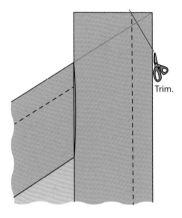

Trim.

Turning the quilt to the other side, with the corner point up, fold in the right side of the corner. On the left side, roll the left edge in to meet the quilt edge. Then fold again to create the miter. Depending on the way you hold the quilt when hand finishing, you may need to pre-fold the corners and pin in place.

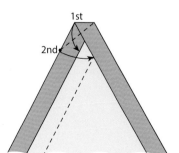

1st

2nd

INSIDE MITERED CORNERS

Traditional designs such as double wedding ring and scalloped curves have inside corners. These can be faced. However, for the effort that is put into the quilt, it would be better to bind them so the edges do not wear out as fast.

After the quilting, trim the batting and backing at the quilt edge. Either staystitch the entire quilt or at least 1˝ on either side of each inside corner. Clip to the stitching within ⅟₁₆˝ or so. Be careful to not cut the stitching.

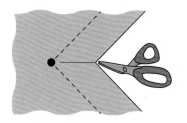

When applying the binding, before the corner, stop and mark the pivot point where the two seam allowances intersect, placing a pin so it is perpendicular to the line of stitching. Stitch to this pivot point and if not exactly at the point, make it be a stitch past. Stop with needle down.

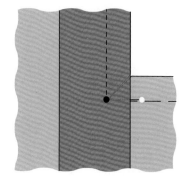

Lift the presser foot, pivot the fabric, and pull the right side straight where the clipped inner corner is. Align the binding raw edges along the edge of the quilt. Pull the fabric on the left side toward the back so that no tucks or folds are in front of the needle. Continue stitching.

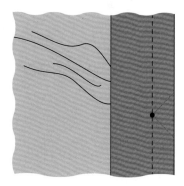

After the binding is attached, at each of the inside corners, clip and trim out the excess binding seam allowance which will match the V shown in the previous diagram.

On the front of the quilt (the side where the binding has been applied), with the edge of the quilt away from you, fold the right side of the binding up and lay the fold to the left flat. Then fold the left side of the miter up.

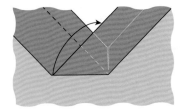

HOLD THE MITER With a blind hem stitch hand sew half of the miter from the center point to the pivot point. Do not sew the entire miter because the other half forms the miter on the back. This can be done later, but it is much easier at this point to get a very neat miter.

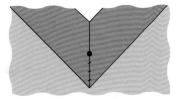

On the back side of the quilt when stitching the binding down, fold the flap to the left through the cut out V. Fold the binding on the right side down and stitch along the right side getting close to the corner.

Bring the fold down to make the mitered corner. Take a couple of stitches at the corner, then blind stitch the miter in place. Continue sewing the binding down.

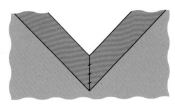

Scallops

Scallops are regular curves that are undulating, like drapes or bunting. The technique of designing a regular curve is applied to a wide border after the quilt is quilted.

Each side of the quilt needs to have full (no partial) scallops. The size scallop chosen needs to fit both dimensions.

For example, a quilt top is 80˝ × 102˝, which includes 9˝ borders. The inside section without borders is 62˝ × 84˝. One third of the width of the border is a good measurement for depth of scallop. Think of how many scallops would look nice per side. The more per side, the curvier the design. For this example, a 12˝ long curve fits 84˝ perfectly, and the extra 2˝ of the 62˝ sides can be accommodated by shifting the curves a bit as needed. So this will be 12˝ curves, 5 on the top and bottom, and 7 on the sides. The corners are designed later.

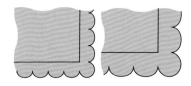

To make a template for the curves, cut a paper rectangle the width of the border by the length of the curve. Mark the depth of the curve on the two ends. Fold this in half, matching these points. Draw a curve from a point to the fold, using a plate, bowl, or other household item to get the desired curve. Cut along the curve through both layers to complete the template.

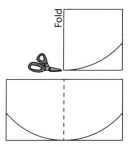

At each corner of the quilt, place a pin the width of the border in from the corner on both sides. On each side, starting at the pin, position one end of the template. Using a removable fabric marking tool, make a mark at the other end, move the template, and repeat. Adjust as needed to extend or shorten a curve or two. Once the marks for the lengths are good, draw the curves.

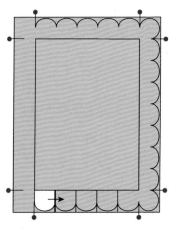

At the corners, place the template aligned with the pin. Draw the curve toward the corner, coming in from both sides. Use these lines to smooth out a desirable curved corner.

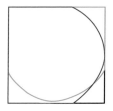

Now cut on the drawn outline. Apply binding following Curved Binding (page 80) and Inside Mitered Corners (page 94).

INSERTED
FINISHES

Each of these finishes places a design element in between the quilt top and the binding. This adds to the look of the finish like a mat on a picture frame. Generally, insertions are narrow to show just an accent of color. That said, the techniques shown here can be changed up to make your project your own style. The Flange and Piping insertions are applied with the same method, slightly different to accommodate the piping. The Lace and Tatting insertions provide a different way to achieve a similar effect, especially with different mediums that don't have seam allowance.

Flange Binding

A flange is a thin strip of fabric that is inserted into a seam.
It is attached to the quilt before adding the binding.

Generally, the finished width of a flange (FL) is ¼˝ or ⅜˝. If you want something thinner, see Faux Flange Binding (page 102). The cut flange strip width (S) needs to be two times the sum of the finished size of the flange plus the seam allowance.

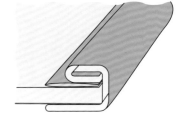

For example: FL is ¼˝, S = 2 (FL + SA) = 2 (¼˝ + ¼˝) = 1˝ flange strip width

Cut the number of straight of grain strips needed for the quilt. The flange can be applied individually to each side with a blunt end. Alternatively, it can be applied with mitered corners. Make lengths for each side, or one continuous strip for mitered corners. Fold the strip in half wrong sides together and press (the flange will not be rolled around to the back so a good pressing will make the task easier).

To apply to each side, align the raw edges of the flange strip with the edge of the quilt. Sew using a slightly narrower seam allowance. At each end, cut the flange strip square to the quilt. Overlap the next flange with the previous one.

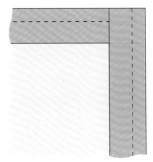

For mitered corners, apply to the entire quilt instead of one side at a time. Begin similar to double fold binding with a 10″ tail and away from the corner (page 53). Align the raw edges of the flange strip with the edge of the quilt. Sew using a slightly narrower seam allowance.

About 3″–4″ from each corner, stop sewing and pre-fold the flange into a miter. This is a reverse of what is done for binding. Have the flange strip flat and smooth to the corner. Then fold the strip under itself to the right on the diagonal.

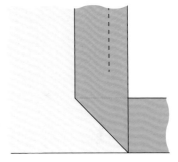

Fold the strip back to the left with the fold at the right edge of the quilt. Align the flange strip with the next edge. This gives a miter on the front. Pin the folds in place and start sewing again, pivoting at the corner and stitching the mitered flange in place.

Work around the quilt. Join the ends of the flange (page 57). Now apply the chosen double fold binding as usual over the flange.

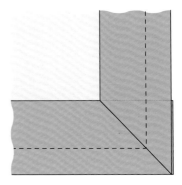

Faux Flange Binding

The narrower the flange the more challenging it is to get it straight and even. With the faux flange that is made from two long strips sewn together and applied like binding, even a small 1/16" strip can be achieved.

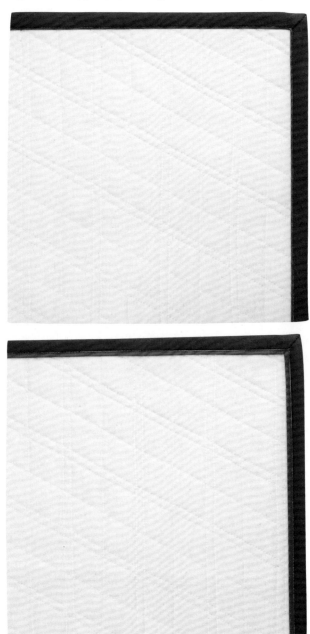

Determine the finished width of the flange you want (FL). Determine the finished width of the binding on the front, F, and back, B. In this method the binding is applied to the back, so the seam allowance will be the same as B. The flange strip is cut wider than the binding strip and is on the inside of the finished binding.

To find the strip widths, figure the double fold binding strip width up to the point before doubling it (T = allowance for quilt thickness). Then add ¼" for the seam allowance to join the two strips. For the flange, take that number and add two times the finished flange width. Here are the formulas for the two strip widths:

W (binding) = SA + B + T + F + ¼" for extra seam.

W (flange) = SA + B + T + F + (2 × FL) + ¼" for extra seam.

Here are two common examples.

For ¼" binding with ⅛" flange:

W (binding) = ¼" + ¼" + ⅛" + ¼" + ¼" = 1⅛" wide binding strips

W (flange) = ¼" + ¼" + ⅛" + ¼" + (2 × ⅛") + ¼" = 1⅜" wide flange strips

For ⅜" binding with ¼" flange: work through the formula and the results are 1½" binding fabric and 2" flange fabric. (Figure the yardage, page 18.)

Sew the binding and flange strips together lengthwise. Press the seam allowance open to reduce the bulk. Follow the instructions for machine finished double fold binding, with the flange side up, applied to the back (page 53). Miter corners and join ends all in a similar manner. Press the binding away from the quilt. When the binding is folded around the edge, the flange sticks out beyond the stitch line. Stitch in the ditch on the flange, from the front.

Stitch in the ditch.

Binding with Piping

Piping adds depth and dimension to the quilt edge. Cording is sewn into a narrow strip, applied to the quilt top, similar to a flange, and then binding is applied over it.

For the piping, purchase enough $1/16''$ or $1/8''$ cording, either cotton or nylon/polyester, for the perimeter of the quilt plus 12″, determined from the length, L, and width, W, of the quilt.

[2 (L + W) + 12″] / 36″. Round up to the nearest ¼ yard.

Piping strips are 1″ wide and can be either crosswise grain or cut on the bias. Here is the yardage for crosswise grain:

[2 (L + W) + 12″] / 40″, round up, + 5″. Divide this number by 36″ and round to the nearest ⅛ yard.

If you prefer bias, for 1″ wide piping strips, depending on how many short pieces are used, a fat quarter yields 120″–250″, and ⅜ yard yields 300″–450″.

Cut the 1″ piping strips and join for the total perimeter plus 12″.

Fold the piping strip in half lengthwise wrong sides together and press lightly so the round cording will fit in neatly. Place the cording inside at the fold, and press the strip against the cording from both sides for a tight fit. Pin or clip to hold the cording in place. Prepare the entire length of piping.

Set up your sewing machine with the needle on the left side of the zipper foot. The needle should be just inside the edge of the foot. Stitch close to the cording.

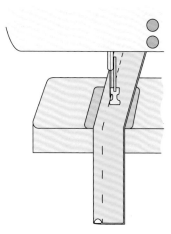

Trim the piping seam allowance to match the binding seam allowance.

EASY TRIMMINGS

To trim the ¼˝ seam allowance on the piping, use Susan Cleveland's Groovin' Piping Trimming Tool or the Add-A-Quarter ruler by CM Designs.

Beginning at a corner, align the raw edge of the piping with the trimmed edge of the quilt. Still working with the zipper foot, stitch as before with the piping up against the zipper foot, and the raw edges aligned. Notice where the raw edge is relative to the other parts of your machine. Pick one or two points where you can guide the edges so that the seams remain straight. This will be used again when applying the binding.

Just before each corner, with the piping flat against the quilt, determine where the pivot point is for mitered corners. At that point from the right, clip the two layers of piping seam allowance up to the stitching. Continue sewing to within one stitch of the pivot point. Stopping with the needle down, lift the presser foot, pivot part way, lower the presser foot, take one stitch on the diagonal, and pivot again so piping is now aligned with the next side.

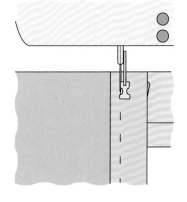
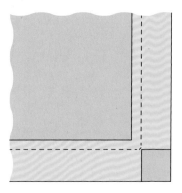

Sew the remaining sides and corners. When back at the first corner, overlap the piping across the previous piping and stitch off the edge of the quilt. Trim these two ends of piping to reduce bulk at this corner. If desired, all the corners can be treated this way.

Continuing to use the zipper foot, apply double fold binding to match the desired finish.

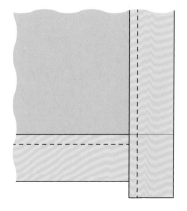

Lace and Tatting

Applying trims can sometimes be done like a traditional flange or piping. However, they generally do not have much seam allowance, if any. In this case, sew the lacework to the binding strip, then apply the binding to the quilt.

Purchase the yardage needed for the perimeter of the quilt plus 10˝. Determine the size of binding to be used. Determine binding yardage required (page 18).

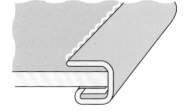

Cut the binding strips to size and join together into one long strip.

Fold the binding wrong sides together with one side shorter by about ⅟₁₆˝. This provides correct placement of the decoration and allows for the roll of the binding around the edge of the quilt.

With the binding strip right side up and the wider side to the left, align the decoration to the left of the fold. Whatever extends to the left of the fold is what will show. Stitch the decoration in place for the length of the binding. With lace, catch the edge using a straight stitch. With tatting, catch the strand of thread at the fold using a blind hem stitch to the right and each wide stitch holding the piece in place.

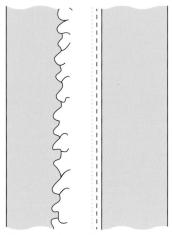

Adding lace to binding

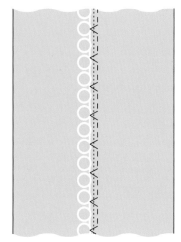

Adding tatting to binding

Apply the binding on the back with the wide side facing the backing and the two raw edges of the binding aligned at the edge of the quilt. Sew with the appropriate seam allowance. Miter the corners as usual. The lace/tatting will fall in place overlapping itself in the corner. Join the ends as usual.

Back

Wrap the binding around to the front. The lace/tatting lays next to the top at the fold of the binding. Machine stitch from the front either in the ditch on the lace/tatting or on the fold of the binding adding a visible line of stitching. This can make the lace/tatting rise up slightly from the quilt, which could be desirable.

EXTENDING FINISHES

These next few finishes are all extensions to the quilt. They are piecework that is added after the quilting is done. Because most of these are considerably larger than binding, they tend to be used on larger quilts. If you are considering one of them on a smaller quilt, it is easier to use the turned method (page 38). Traditionally, on bed quilts, these extensions are only put on the sides and bottom of the quilt.

There are two ways to add these pieces to a quilt. One is traditional and is a variation of the knife-edge finish (page 46). The other incorporates the artist's binding (page 76). The quilting needs to stop ⅝″ in from the edges of the quilt top for both methods. Since the same methods work for all the different design elements, here are the instructions for the two methods.

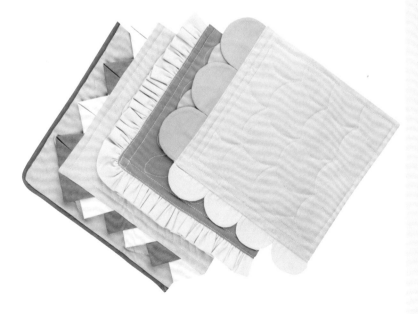

Traditional Using Knife-Edge

Once the layers are quilted, trim the backing and the batting to the edge of the quilt top. Fold back the top and the backing and pin in place, exposing the batting. With rotary cutter, ruler, and mat, trim ¼" more from the batting. Be very careful to not cut the front or back fabrics. The straight line from cutting with a ruler will help create the straight finish.

Place the design element (prairie points, ruffles, petals, or baubles) right sides together and raw edges aligned with the quilt top. Pin in place to be sure spacing is correct. At the corners, the finished edge of the element is at the point where both seam allowances cross.

Note: This will be backwards from how it will be viewed on the front of the quilt. Baste in place with a large stitch length just inside the seam allowance, less than ¼" from the edges. Once positioned as needed, with a regular stitch length, sew the ¼" seam allowance.

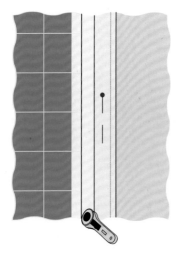

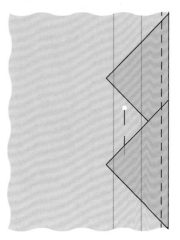

Unpin the top and backing. Fold batting and backing to the back of the quilt at the ⅝" line. Pin in place so that the edge of the quilt top is free.

With the top pulled out of the way, fold ¼″ of the backing over the batting. Press in place. At the corners, fold the backing on a diagonal, then fold and press each side in like a miter. Depending on the design element, carefully trim on the diagonal at the corner to reduce bulk.

Turn the quilt over, align the fold of backing and batting to the stitch line of the design element, and pin in place. This can be hand stitched or machine stitched close to the edge to hold the backing down. If done by machine, a second row of stitching ¼″ away adds extra strength to the edge and finishes the design off nicely.

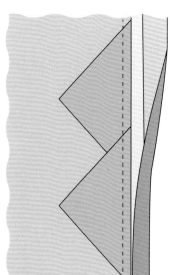
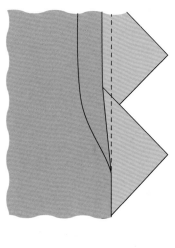

MIND THE GAP There is a gap from the thick seam allowance to the quilted area. Fold the batting back on itself so it fills the gap. Pin and stitch as usual.

Easier Way Using Artist's Binding

This method has a strip of fabric used to secure the seam allowance to the back just like the artist's binding. For straight sides, these are 1½˝ strips about 4˝ longer than the length of each side. For curved edges, this is a 1½˝ wide continuous bias strip that is the length of the perimeter of the quilt plus 10˝. Figure the yardage (page 18). Cut the strips and join them together for each side. Or make one long continuous bias strip for curves (page 24). With wrong sides together, fold and press the strip(s) in half lengthwise.

With the quilting at least ⅝˝ away from the edge of the quilt, trim the backing and the batting to the edge of the quilt top. Fold back the top, pinning if necessary. Trim ½˝ more off the batting and backing. Be very careful to not cut the quilt top.

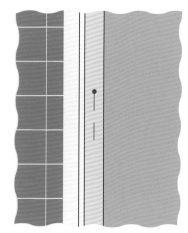

For straight sides, work one side at a time. For curved edges, work in 2–4 foot sections. Place the design element(s), right sides together with the quilt top, starting and stopping at the corners at the pivot point where both seams cross. Pin as needed. This will be backwards from how it will be viewed on the front of the quilt. Once the spacing of the design elements is correct, baste in place just inside the seam allowance, less than ¼˝.

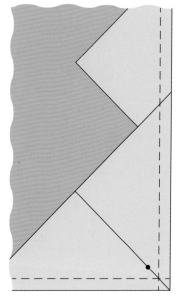

Place the artist binding strip on top of the design element with raw edges aligned. For straight sides, with a regular stitch length, starting just after the pivot point with a back stitch, sew the strip in place with a ¼" seam allowance. At the corner, stop just before the pivot point of the seam allowance in from both sides. Pivot perpendicular to the seam and sew off the quilt edge. Trim the excess binding strip at the edge of the quilt. Repeat on each side. Clip the batting and backing on the diagonal.

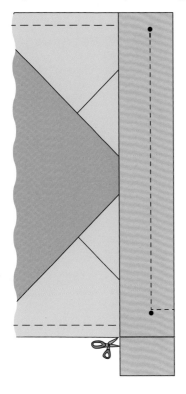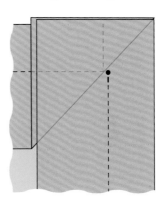

Roll the binding strip to the back over the batting and backing, folding the loose ends back at the corners. The seam allowance of the quilt top and added elements will fill in the space to the batting and backing. The pivot point is at the very corner of the finished quilt. Overlap or miter the ends of the binding strips. Press the binding in place. Hand or machine stitch along the folds.

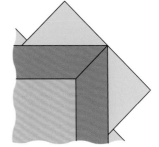

Piping on the Edge

When piping is the only edge, there needs to be strength in such a narrow strip holding the entire design together. To be sure it is seen and worth the effort, you want to work with ³⁄₁₆˝ or thicker cording.

Front

Back

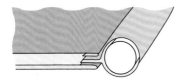

For piping, purchase enough ³⁄₁₆˝ or larger cording, either cotton or nylon/polyester, for the perimeter of the quilt, plus 12˝.

To prepare your piping, refer to Piping (page 104). Once the piping is prepared, trim the seam allowance so it is ¼˝ from the stitching line to the raw edge.

Add the piping either the knife-edge way (page 110), or the artist's binding way (page 112).

Use the following method to join the ends. Where the ends meet, rip out the basting stitches around the cording back to where the seam allowances begin and end. Pull the cording out of the fold. Join the strip ends like double fold binding (page 57). Put the cording back in the binding. Trim the cording ends so they meet halfway. Stitch this remaining section to the quilt top.

Cross section where ends meet

Prairie Points

Prairie points are a classic design element for quilting. They are squares of fabric folded into triangles and attached to the edge of the quilt.

Front

There are two ways to make prairie points: individual squares and continuous strips. Individual squares folded into triangles can be varying colors and sizes and can be easily adjusted to fit the quilt. The continuous strip method is faster to make and has the advantage of the points already being attached to each other. However, because of this, it can be challenging to adjust the position of the points.

There are also two styles of prairie points based on how they are folded. One is based on a horizontal fold, the other on a diagonal fold. Both styles can be made using either technique. To see what will work best, read through the section and then choose.

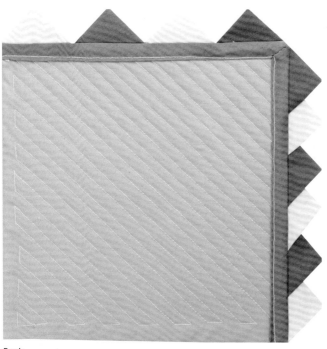

Back

Back

The first step is to decide what size the prairie points are going to be. Common sizes, depth × length, are 1″ × 2″, 1¼″ × 2½″, and 1½″ × 3″. To figure the size square to cut (S), take the length of the prairie point, P, and add ½″ for the seam allowances. These three example sizes need 2½″, 3″, and 3½″ squares, respectively. Of course, other sizes are possible. For our example, of a 55″ × 72″ quilt top with 1″ × 2″ prairie points, we use 2½″ squares.

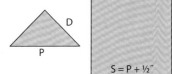

Now that we know the size of the prairie point and the square, S, we need to figure out how many to make, M, and how much yardage to buy. Measure the length, L, and width, W, of the quilt top finished size. Divide both of these measurements by the finished length of the prairie point and round to the nearest whole number. This is the number that can fit side by side. Prairie points can be overlapped by enough to use up to twice as many. Any more than this becomes too bulky in the seam allowance.

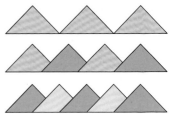

Using square size, S, length of quilt, L, and width of quilt, W, the number of prairie points to make, M is 2 (L/P + W/P) up to 4 (L/P + W/P) where each of the divisions are rounded up.

Example: M = 2 (55″/2″) + 2 (72″/2″) = 128 up to 256

Here is a chart for how many prairie points (from individual squares or continuous strips) can be made from different yardages. For our example we need at least ¾ yard and at most 1⅜. If using multiple fabrics like the photo shows, divide the yardage as needed.

Yield from Yardage for Prairie Points

FINISHED SIZE	SIZE OF SQUARE	¼ YARD	⅜ YARD	½ YARD	¾ YARD	1 YARD
1″ × 2″	2½″	48	80	112	160	224
1¼″ × 2½″	3″	26	52	65	104	143
1½″ × 3″	3½″	22	33	55	77	110

INDIVIDUAL SQUARES

Folded Horizontally

When these are individual squares, quite often they are placed next to each other rather than overlapped but it is not a strict rule. For each prairie point, fold the square in half horizontally, wrong sides together. Press. Then fold each corner on the fold, down to the center of the raw edge. Press well. Make the number needed for the project.

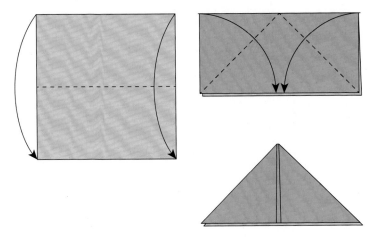

Decide how the prairie points will be placed along each side of the quilt. If they are going to be side-by-side, they overlap in the seam allowance by ½˝ so that when the seam allowance is sewn, the prairie points just touch. If you are going to overlap the prairie points, determine the desired spacing. Baste them together in the seam allowance into sections that can be applied as a single unit. Follow the instructions to apply extending elements to the quilt (page 110), overlapping slightly if needed to make them match at the corners of the quilt.

Folded Diagonally

These prairie points are nested and can be overlapped up to half their length. For each prairie point, fold a fabric square in half on the diagonal. Press. Fold in half so the two corners on the fold meet. Press well.

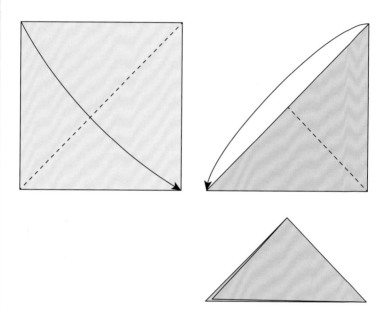

Decide how the points will be placed along each side of the quilt. Baste them in sections that can then be applied as a long strip. On each section, leave the last point open so it can nest with the next section. Follow the instructions to apply extending elements to the quilt (page 110). Adjust the sections to make them fit the quilt top.

CONTINUOUS STRIPS

The prairie points are made as units from double wide strips. The squares are marked on each side of the center fold, with one side shifted by half of a square. Cut crosswise grain or bias strips that are twice the width of the prairie point square. The strip lengths total the length of each side of the quilt. For an even number of points, cut a multiple of the square size. For an odd number of points, use a multiple of the square size plus a half square. Cut enough strips for each side. For example, cut 2 strips 5˝ × 40˝ and 2 strips 5˝ × 15˝ for the top and bottom edges of the quilt. Cut 6 strips 5˝ × 25˝, 3 for each side. They can be adjusted down to 72˝ with overlapping or with trimming down by one square. Press the strips in half, wrong sides together. Open the strips and then mark the lines shown in the diagram and cut with scissors or measure with a ruler and rotary cut to the center fold. With the end of the ruler at the fold, stop cutting when the blade is at the end of the ruler. Note that the last prairie point can be on either side to get an even or odd number per strip. Snip out the half square on each end.

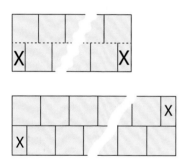

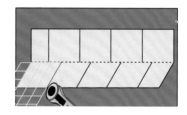

Folded Horizontally

With the strip right side down, fold each square into the center line, keeping cut edges aligned. Do not let the square extend across the center line. Repeat this on both sides for all the sections.

For each square on one side of the strip, fold down both corners into the center aligning the raw edges with the center fold. Press well.

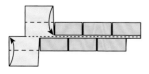

Turn the strip over so the right side of the strip is up. On the other half of the strip, for each square, fold down both corners into the center, aligning the raw edges with the center line. Press well.

Fold the sides together for an alternating front back arrangement. This is my favorite because of the layers and design lines. Stitch along the seam allowance edge with a large basting stitch.

Overlap the ends of the strips and/or remove a prairie point as needed to continue the design and fit the quilt top. Follow the instructions for applying extended elements to the quilt top (page 110).

- -

Folded Diagonally

With the strip right side down, starting at the right end (left for left-handed), along the top row, for each square, fold the upper right corner down to the lower left corner of the square keeping one edge aligned to the left edge of the square and the other aligned at the center line. Press well. Repeat for the lower row, folding the lower right to the upper left, with edges aligned to the left edge of the square and to the center line. These folds go the same direction for the length of the strip.

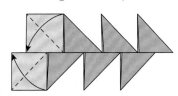

left point of each square, up to the right to the fold line, aligning the folds on the right.

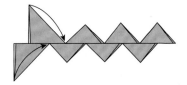

Working from either direction, nest a point from the upper row inside one from the lower row and vice versa. Pin in place on an ironing surface and press well. Stitch along the seam allowance edge with a large basting stitch, leaving the last prairie point open.

On the top row, fold the upper left point of each square, down to the right to the fold line, aligning the folds on the right. Repeat for the lower row, folding the lower

Insert the beginning of a new strip into this end to make the units fit the quilt top. Follow the instructions for applying extending elements to a quilt (page 110).

Ruffles

The size of ruffles needs to balance with the project. They can be a single layer of fabric with a narrow hem, gathered a lot, or a double layer, folded and gathered less. Here are some samples all made with standard quilter's cotton:

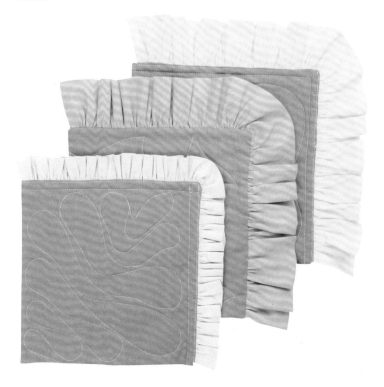

Once you have decided on the style of the ruffles, figure the yardages required.

D = finished depth of ruffle

R = width of strip to cut. For single layer: R = D + ½″ (hem) + ¼″ (SA). For double layer: R = 2 (D + ¼″ (SA))

M = amount of ruffling (multiply by 2, 2½, 3)

P = perimeter = 2 (L + W). If adding ruffles to only 3 sides, perimeter = W + 2 L

C = length for corners. C = 4 × (2 × D) = 8 D, or 4 D for 3 sides

S = number of strips to cut, S = M (P + C)/40″; round up to next whole number

Y = yardage to buy. Y = S × R/36″ (round up to nearest ⅛ yd) + ¼ yard extra

For example, for a 52″ × 74″ quilt, single layer, 1½″ finished (2¼″ strip) with 2½ times ruffling, the yardage is figured as follows:

D = 1½″

P = 252″, C = 12″, R = 2¼″, M = 2½

S = 2½ × (252″ + 12″) / 40″ = 16½, round up to 17 strips

Y = 17 × 2¼″ / 36″ (rounded up) + ¼ yard extra = 1⅜ yards

Cut the number of strips required for your project.

For a single layer ruffle, join the strips on their short ends into one large loop, using French seams if desired (see below). If only ruffling 3 sides, join into one long strip. Finish one long edge (and the ends if ruffling 3 sides) with ¼″ narrow hems.

For a double layer, join the strips on their short ends into one long loop with seams pressed open. If only ruffling 3 sides, join into one long strip. Fold in half and press. If only ruffling 3 sides, fold and press in ¼″ on the ends, then fold the strip in half and press. To finish the ends, stitch ⅛″ along each end.

French seams French seams are made to hide raw edges inside the seam. When a seam might be exposed, this is how it is "hidden". With **wrong** sides together, sew the seam slightly narrower than the finished seam will be.

Press seam to one side. Trim any frayed edges. Fold fabrics right sides together enclosing the seam. Now sew the seam as usual.

Mark the four center points of the edges of the quilt top. Fold the prepared ruffle into fourths and mark these points. Each of these sections will be treated separately and applied to one fourth of the quilt.

If only three sides have ruffles, mark the center point on both the ruffle and the bottom edge of the quilt. Each section of the ruffle will be distributed along one side and one half of the lower edge of the quilt.

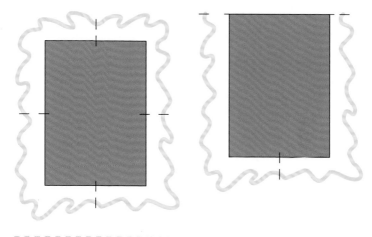

Between two marked points of the ruffle, within the seam allowance, sew a zigzag stitch over a narrow cording, string, or thick thread for drawing up the ruffle. Be careful to not stitch the cording. Use a 1.5mm or 17spi stitch length for a more even ruffle with less puckers. Leave 6˝–10˝ of cording on each end of the section. Sew the drawstring into each section.

For each section, begin drawing up the gathers. Work the fabric down along the cording. Work from both ends averaging out the amount of ruffles throughout. Be careful to not let the drawstring be pulled out at either end. I wrap it around a pin, once I know that I am finished working that end of the ruffle. Get the ruffles gathered close to the size needed for the quilt.

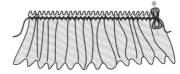

Now apply the ruffle to the quilt following the instructions for inserted elements (page 110). At the corners gather the ruffles tighter so that there is enough fabric to lay flat at the outer edge of the ruffle.

Petals

Petals are easy because they can be overlapped like prairie points and adjusted to fit the length and width of the quilt. Here are a few variations of petals.

Front

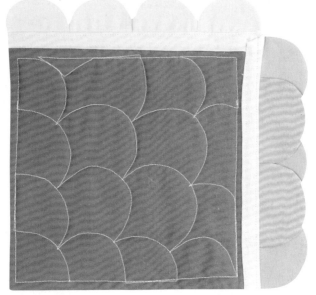

Back

"Baubles" are a fun variation.

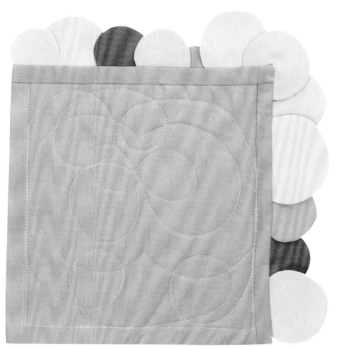

Back

An easy shape to use is a half-circle with ¼˝ seam allowances added all around. For a petal that is 1½˝ × 3˝ finished, use 2˝ × 3½˝ rectangles.

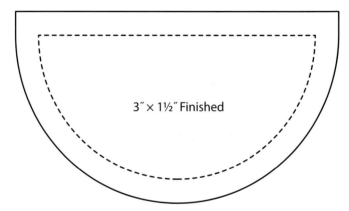

3˝ × 1½˝ Finished

Decide what type of overlap you want and figure the number of petals that you will need. Remember there is a front and back to the shape, so you need 2 fabric pieces for each petal. Figure yardage as follows:

P = 2 × number of petals needed

N = number of petal rectangles (length) from 40˝ strip

S = number of strips to cut. S = P/N; round up to next whole number

Y = yardage to buy. Y = S × width of petal rectangles / 36˝ + ¼ yard extra

Cut pairs of rectangles the size needed for the petal. Draw the design and sew along the stitching line using shorter stitches, 1.5mm or 17 spi, for tight curves. Leave the straight side open for turning and the seam allowance. Trim and clip curves. Turn and press. If desired, top stitch around the edge for a crisp finish.

If the petals will be overlapped, arrange as desired and staystitch together in the seam allowance to create sections. By having a few sections, they can be adjusted slightly to fit when placing them on the quilt. Follow the instructions for applying inserted elements to a quilt (page 110).

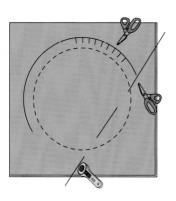

BAUBLES For the bauble design, using two layers of fabric, right sides together, sew various size circles using 1.0mm or 25 spi, leaving enough fabric on the outside for a seam allowance.

1. Cut off a section of the circle to create a straight edge and an opening.

2. Trim the remaining fabric to $\frac{1}{8}˝$ seam allowance.

3. Clip, clip, and clip the curve. Turn each bauble inside out and smooth the curves. Overlap and apply to the project.

PROJECTS
FOR PRACTICE

Quilter's Pocketbook

FINISHED SIZE: 4½″ × 6″

The Quilter's Pocketbook is the perfect way to keep your scissors, needles, thread, and thimble all together ready for sewing. It is a perfect gift to make for your crafting friends, and you practice binding techniques in the process! They are so fun to create, you will find yourself gathering fabrics and buttons to match before you know it.

Materials

FABRICS

Main fabric (outside and pocket): ¼ yard or 9″ × 12″

Lining fabric (inside): ¼ yard or 6″ × 9″

Binding fabric: ⅛ yard

Felt or wool: 3″ × 3″

Batting: 9″ × 12″

OTHER SUPPLIES

¼″ × ½″ piece of hook and loop tape

½″–¾″ button, shank style

1¼ yards of ¼″ double faced satin or grosgrain ribbon

NOTES ABOUT THE BINDING

Choose either ⅜″ hand finished applied to the outside or ⅜″ machine finished applied to the inside, as described for double fold binding, page 51. Both use 2¼″ wide strips as shown here.

⅜″, hand-finished, seam allowance aligned with quilt top, batting trimmed ⅛″ beyond: S = 2 (¼″ + ⅜″ + ⅜″ + ⅛″) = 2¼″

⅜″, machine-finished, ¼″ on back: S = 2 (¼″ + ⅜″ + ¼″ + ⅛″ + *⅛″) = 2¼″

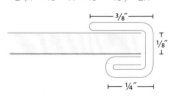

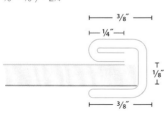

Cutting

MAIN FABRIC
1 rectangle 6″ × 9″
2 rectangles 3½″ × 4½″ (pocket)

LINING FABRIC
1 rectangle 6″ × 9″

BINDING FABRIC
1 strip 2¼″ × width of fabric

BATTING
1 rectangle 6″ × 9″

RIBBON
1 piece each at 13″, 12″, 8″, and 4″
with diagonal cuts to prevent
fraying

Preparing the Main Body

Fold and press the lining in half to mark the stitch line. Fold the 13″ ribbon in half and sew it 1½″ down and 1″ in from the upper right-hand corner. Reinforce with back stitching. Sew the loop tape at 3″ down and 3″ over from the upper right-hand corner.

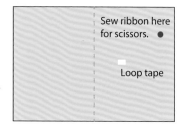

On one pocket piece, measuring from the front, sew the hook tape at ½″ down and 3″ in from the left-hand side.

Trim the felt square into an octagon if desired by snipping off the four corners. Sew the felt/wool to the lining centered on the left side using a decorative stitch or straight stitch.

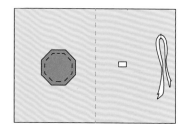

Preparing the Pocket

Layer the pocket pieces, right sides together. Stitch on two sides, near the hook tape and across the top. Clip the corner, turn and press (page 41).

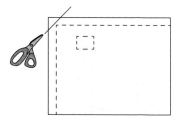

Layer the main body rectangle, right side down, the batting piece, and the prepared lining, right side up. Pin together. Stitch along the fold at the center through all three layers. Place the pocket on top of the lining with the lower and right edges aligned. Check that the hook tape matches the loop tape. The pocket should not overlap the center line. Stitch ⅛″ along the left and right edges of the pocket through all layers, reinforcing at the top edge with back stitches.

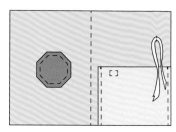

To make two pockets, one for thimbles and the other for scissors, at 2″ from the right, sew through all layers from the top edge, reinforcing with a back stitch, to the bottom edge of the pocket. Baste around the outer edge of the body through all thicknesses in the seam allowance.

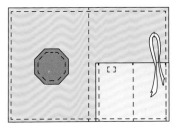

Adding the Ribbons

Pin the ends of the 12″ ribbon at the top and 8″ ribbon at the bottom of the center line. Staystitch in place.

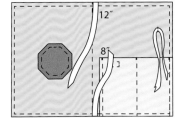

Keep the loose ends of the ribbons free by either pinning them in the middle of lining or tucking them into the thimble pocket.

Trim the 4″ ribbon to 3″ for a ½″ button and 3½″ for a ⅝″ button. Fold the ribbon in half to make a loop. On the main side of the body, pin the ends of the ribbon loop to the center near the pocket. Baste through all thicknesses.

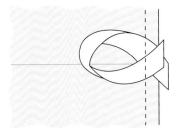

Binding

Apply double fold binding on the main side for hand finishing and on the lining side for machine finishing (page 53). Start on the bottom edge on the pocket. This provides enough space to sew the join so that it will be on the back of the project when it is folded shut.

CLOSE CORNERS When mitering the corner just before the join, pin - do not sew - the miter in place. Find the critical point where the ends need to meet. Then unpin the miter, sew the two ends together, refold the miter, and finish stitching the binding down. A few extra steps but well worth it!

Finishing

Fold the ribbon loop around from the back to the front and mark where the button should be sewn. Sew the button just inside the binding. Voila! The project is done.

To outfit your Quilter's Pocketbook, place needles in the felt patch, tie thread onto the ribbons in the middle, tie scissors into the right pocket, and place a thimble and clips in the left pocket. Now you have what you need to hand finish those projects that deserve some extra special attention.

Pot Holder or Hot Pad

FINISHED SIZE: 6˝ × 8˝

This project demonstrates how the width of the binding strip is affected by the thickness of the batting, and also offers an opportunity to practice finishing simple curved corners. With all the layers needed to provide heat protection, we definitely have to add in a little extra fabric to the width of the binding strips. Pot holders are great for using fat quarters, and for practicing machine quilting on a domestic, home machine. I have included instructions for making 4 pot holders at once in parentheses (like this).

Materials

Front: 6˝ × 8˝ (1 fat quarter , cut into 4 pieces 6˝ × 8˝)

Back: 7˝ × 9˝ (1 fat quarter)

Middle*: 7˝ × 9˝ (1 fat quarter)

Binding: 1 fat quarter (½ yard)

Cotton batting**: 2 rectangles 7˝ × 9˝ (2 rectangles 14˝ × 18˝)

Heat-resistant thermal batting**: 7˝ × 9˝ (14˝ × 18˝)

* This unseen layer of fabric is used when quilting the batting and backing together. Lines of stitching can transfer heat, so the front fabric is left unstitched except for the binding.

** Or layers of cotton batting totaling ¼˝ thick.

NOTES ABOUT THE BINDING

With the ½˝ binding on the front and ⅜˝ on the back for the machine finish, and thick batting of ¼˝, the strip width was figured to be:

$S = 2(SA + F + B + T)$

$= 2(⅜˝ + ½˝ + ⅜˝ + ¼˝)$

$= 3˝$

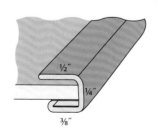

Construction

Layer the middle, 2 layers of cotton batting, thermal batting, and backing, and quilt as desired. I recommend including one line of stitching down the middle in the shorter direction. It helps the pot holder fold easily when in use.

Pin the wrong side of the front piece(s) to the middle fabric of the quilted unit. Slowly baste through all layers in the seam allowance. Avoid puckers at the curves or at the quilting lines. Or throw caution to the wind—it's a pot holder!

Trim through all layers to make the pot holder(s) 6˝ × 8˝. On the back side, the upper right corner has the hanging loop. Use a coffee mug or similar sized circle as a template to mark a curve on the other three corners. Trim with scissors.

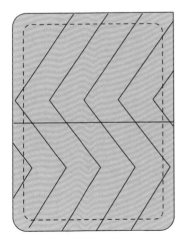

Cut 3˝ wide bias strips from the binding fabric. Piece together to make a 35˝ length (4 lengths 3˝ × 35˝ or 140˝ continuous binding).

Fold the strip in half as it is being applied. Begin at the square corner of the pot holder. Leaving a 4˝ tail and beginning ½˝ in from the edge, apply double fold binding. Refer to instructions for applying binding to the back of the piece to be machine-finished (page 53) and curved binding (page 80).

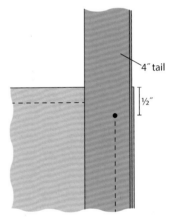

4˝ tail

½˝

When you are a couple of inches away from the square corner, fold the initial tail of fabric out of the way. Continue stitching the binding to the corner. Cut any remaining binding strip off at the end. Fold the beginning tail into fourths lengthwise, halfway in from both sides and then in half again. Stitch along the fold to the edge of the pot holder.

Press binding toward the edge, fold to the front, and press in place. From the front, machine stitch along the fold. At the corner, twist the tail a half turn and either tuck it into the last bit of open binding to be sewn or simply stitch the end down to the binding with reinforced stitching like the sample.

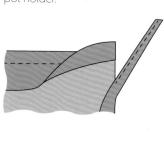

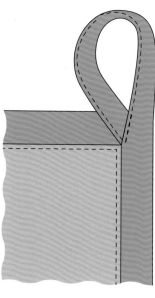

Place Mats

FINISHED SIZE: 12″ × 18″

Pick fun, festive fabrics for your set of four new place mats. There are many ways to get a wide binding with a tradeoff between ease and amount of fabric. This technique has a wide seam allowance for easy alignment of the fabrics when sewing and uses the single fold method to save fabric. To make this quick and easy, we will finish by machine. Have fun adding these methods to your binding skills.

Materials (for 4 place mats)

Front: ⅞ yard

Back: ⅞ yard

Binding fabric: 1⅝ yards

Batting: 30″ × 42″

NOTES ABOUT THE BINDING

With the 1½″ binding on the front and 1⅜″ on the back for the machine finish, the strip width was figured to be:

$$S = 2F + 2B + T = 2(1\tfrac{1}{2}″) + 2(1\tfrac{3}{8}″) + \tfrac{1}{8}″ = 5\tfrac{7}{8}″$$

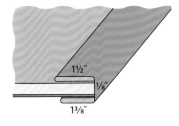

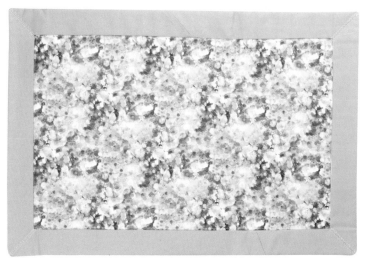

Construction

Layer the front, batting, and backing fabric, and quilt as desired. Cut into 4 place mats 12″ × 18″.

Cut 8 strips 5⅞″ × WOF of binding fabric.

For each place mat follow these steps:

Join two binding strips (page 26). Apply the strip to a quilted 12″ × 18″ mat following the instructions for machine-finished wide binding (page 70) and for machine-finished single fold binding (page 65). Align the single layer of binding with the edge of the back side of the place mat. Begin sewing just before the corner on one long side. End sewing just after the other corner

on that same side. Sew with a 1⅜″ seam allowance in from the edge. Fold and miter the corners at 1⅜″ in from both sides.

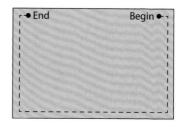

When joining the ends, the critical point is at 1⅜″ in from the edge.

Press binding toward the place mat edge, fold to the front, and press with the other edge folded in. Machine stitch the binding.

Way Back When

Wide bindings started for me when I put a 1″ binding on a baby quilt because I thought a ¼″ wouldn't be sufficient and I didn't want to add one more border. Am I lazy or crazy?! I have put wide bindings on many of my quilts to repeat a 1″ inner border or other element in the quilt, like the log cabin strip width shown here.

Wide bindings really make a statement. Watch for opportunities to use these larger-than-life finishes.

Table Runner

FINISHED SIZE: 13˝ × 70˝

Have you avoided any quilt design that had corners that weren't square? With this table runner, you learn how easy it is to bind angles different than 90 degrees. The project has no piecing so we can focus on the binding instruction. The cutting is for angles other than 90 degrees, both more and less.

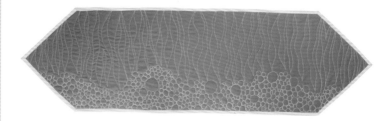

Materials

Front: 2 yards

Back: 2¼ yards

Binding: ⅝ yard

Batting: 19˝ × 80˝

NOTES ABOUT THE BINDING

This project has a ½˝ finished width for the front binding. The binding is made with 2¾˝ strips for machine finishing. The width was figured as follows with the seam allowance (SA), front (F), back (B) and batting thickness (T):

$$S = 2 (SA + F + B + T) = 2 (⅜˝ + ½˝ + ⅜˝ + ⅛˝) = 2¾˝$$

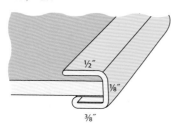

THE QUILT BINDING BIBLE

Cut seven 2¾˝ × WOF strips of binding. Join together into one long strip (page 26).

> ### MAKE IT YOURS, TIMES THREE
>
> A typical table runner is 13˝–16˝ wide. With 40˝ or wider fabric, 2 yards of front fabric and 2¼ yards of backing fabric will be enough for three runners, one for you, one for your best friend, and one for the guild bazaar. If you decide to do this, purchase 3 times the binding and have the batting the same size as the backing. Layer and quilt the yardage of top, batting, and backing, and then cut each individual table runner, ready for shaping and binding.

CUSTOMIZING THE SIZE This project can be made in any length or width. Determine the yardage for the length of the front. You will need backing and batting that is at least 4˝ wider and longer than the finished size. Follow the instructions to craft your very own custom-made table runner.

Binding yardage = (Perimeter/40˝, rounded up to nearest whole number) +1) × binding strip width / 36˝. Round up to nearest ⅛ or ¼ yard.

Construction

For a single 13˝ × 70˝ runner, cut a rectangle from the front fabric measuring 13˝ × length of fabric. Refer to the instructions on how to fold extra-long pieces and cut using a 24˝ ruler (page 23).

Cut the backing in a similar manner at 17˝ wide if quilting by hand or by home machine, or 19˝ wide if quilting by longarm machine.

Cut the batting slightly larger than the front. Layer front, batting, and backing, baste and quilt as desired.

Trim batting and backing to match the rectangle shape of the top. Measuring from the ends, on both edges of the runner, make a mark 9˝ from each corner. Fold the rectangle in half lengthwise and mark the center point at each end. Draw lines from the center point to the 2 marks 9˝ from the end. Repeat for the other end. Rotary cut along these lines for the finished shape of the table runner.

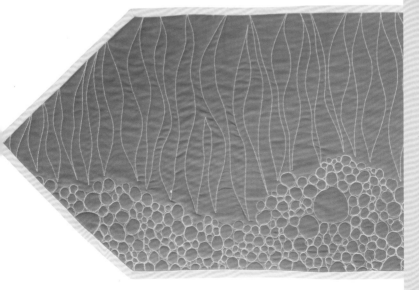

Apply the binding to the runner back as a double fold binding with a ⅜"
seam allowance (page 53). At the corners, use instructions for wide angles
and narrow angles (pages 90 and 92). Note that corner binding folds will
not align with the previous side, rather they will be perpendicular to the
new side.

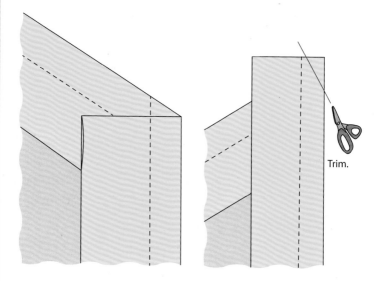

Trim.

Join the ends (page 57).

Complete the binding as described for machine finished double fold
binding, (page 59).

ABOUT THE AUTHOR

Recognized internationally for her expertise in quilting, Marci enjoys sharing ideas that simplify the quilting process. A native of Dallas, Texas, Marci began teaching quilting in 1989 for her local quilting guild and shops. In 1993, she started Alicia's Attic, a company that combines her love of math and teaching with her love of quilting.

As an admirer of traditional quilts, Marci was inspired to author the Not Your Grandmother's Flower Garden series, which uses traditional patterns that people associate with grandmothers but simplifies the techniques.

Contact Marci at marci@quiltmb.com.
Follow Marci on social media:
Website: quiltwithmarcibaker.com
Facebook: QuiltMB
YouTube: @MarciBaker
Instagram: QuiltwithMarciBaker

In 2006, she began collaborating with Sara Nephew, another 60° designer, and they have now published four books together. With the new business name, Quilt with Marci Baker, she teaches these designs both traveling and on C&T's online learning platform, Creative Spark. Always thinking of new ideas, Marci has branched out with several projects of her own. Keep an eye out for more to come!

Marci and her husband, Clint, live in Fort Collins, CO, where they enjoy the beautiful mountain views. And every now and then she gets back to Texas to visit family and friends.

CREATIVE SPARK

ONLINE LEARNING

Quilting courses to become an expert quilter...

From their studio to yours, Creative Spark instructors are teaching you how to create and become a master of your craft. So not only do you get a look inside their creative space, you also get to be a part of engaging courses that would typically be a one or multi-day workshop from the comfort of your home.

Creative Spark is not your one-size-fits-all online learning experience. We welcome you to be who you are, share, create, and belong.

Scan for a gift from u

creativespark.ctpub.com